D1259777

the Power
of Paws

the Power *of* Paws

Reflections on a Life with Dogs

GARY SHIEBLER

Foreword by
Kimberly Williams-Paisley

THE LYONS PRESS
Guilford, CT
An imprint of The Globe Pequot Press

To buy books in quantity for corporate use
or incentives, call **(800) 962–0973,**
or e-mail **premiums@GlobePequot.com.**

Copyright © 2008 by Gary Shiebler

ALL RIGHTS RESERVED. No part of this book may be reproduced or transmitted
in any form by any means, electronic or mechanical, including photocopying and
recording, or by any information storage and retrieval system, except as may be
expressly permitted in writing from the publisher. Requests for permission should
be addressed to The Globe Pequot Press, Attn: Rights and Permissions Department,
P.O. Box 480, Guilford CT 06437.

The Lyons Press is an imprint of The Globe Pequot Press.

Photo on page 28 courtesy of New England Old English Sheepdog Rescue, Inc.,
www.neoesr.org

All other photos courtesy of the author.

Text design by Claire Zoghb

Library of Congress Cataloging-in-Publication Data

Shiebler, Gary.
The power of paws : reflections on a life with dogs / Gary Shiebler.
p. cm.
ISBN 978-1-59921-309-5 (alk. paper)
1. Dogs—Anecdotes. 2. Dog owners—Anecdotes.
3. Human-animal relationships—Anecdotes. I. Title.
SF426.2.S538 2008
636.7—dc22
2007050102

Printed in the United States of America

10 9 8 7 6 5 4 3 2 1

FOR MY MOTHER AND FATHER,

who've supported me through every
harebrained plan and scheme my
restless mind has put forward and for
teaching me to measure love not by
what we say but by what we do.

Contents

Foreword

I HAVE NOT ALWAYS BEEN A DOG PERSON. When I was growing up, my siblings and I were told we were allergic to dogs, not so much because we *were* allergic to them, but because I don't think my parents wanted to deal with taking care of one. Dogs were smelly, slobbery, in-your-face messes of energy, and no one in my family could understand why everyone was so crazy about these creatures.

Then we got one.

I was really itching to have a baby about three years after my husband and I got married. Around that time, a friend of mine brought her Cavalier King Charles Spaniel puppy into work. I instantly fell in love with the little ball of fur. Lucy snuggled in my lap for an hour, and I almost cried when I had to give her back. I went home to my husband and told him how much I wanted to get a puppy. Because he wasn't ready for a family—and because he'd always secretly wanted a dog—he was all for it.

One of the first things Holler, our new puppy, did when we took him home was pee on the carpet. I didn't care. I gave him water out of the little cap of my water bottle, and took a dozen pictures of him as he drank, ate, ran in circles, and chewed up my shoes. Whenever he slept, I lay there next to him—watching his little paws twitch, trying to imagine the dreams he was having. And in those first few months, I got up many times in the middle of the night to check on him and make sure he was still breathing, not unlike what I do now with my own child. We taught him how to sit, fetch, shake, and lie down on his side when we "shot" him with a make-believe gun. Almost immediately, Holler changed our lives. He made us better people. I took him on long walks and actually met some of my neighbors for the first time, and got to know their dogs.

Eventually, my husband and I started fostering dogs from Happy Tales Humane Society in Franklin, Tennessee, and became much more aware of the problems associated with mistreated and neglected animals. Some of those dogs we will never forget. Today, Holler is just as much a valued member of the family as anyone in this house. I can't imagine the last day of his life.

So now I adore dogs, and I absolutely love all of the stories within these pages. Gary Shiebler appreciates the unique and humble power each dog has over its owner: That of pure, impassioned, and unwavering love. To him, each dog is a hero in its own unique way and deserves to be celebrated as such. He makes me wish I had been a dog person right from the start. But he's inspired me to spend a good part of the rest of my life trying to catch up.

—*Kimberly Williams-Paisley*

Acknowledgments

To my beloved wife, Linda, and daughter, Hayden. You know the mess I'd be in without you.

To my brother and best friend, Glenn.

To my sister, Susan, and her amazing kids—Michael, Elissa, Matthew, and Christa.

To my manager, Connie Nelson, as good a friend as anyone could ask for.

To all my friends, musicians, songwriters in Nashville and beyond (in no particular order): Jimmy and Pat Johnson; Mike Baker; Martin Parker; Deanie Richardson; Buck and Kathy Jarrell; Tim Atwood; Marcia Ramirez; Craig Campbell; Bobby and Jeannie Bare; Ralph and Joy Emery; Evelyn Shriver; Susan Nadler; Michael Campbell; George and Nancy Jones; Porter and Deb Wagoner; Little Jimmy and Mona Dickens; Jerry Reed; Patty Loveless; Frank Mull; Merle, Theresa, and Ben Haggard; Amy Nelson; Tanya Tucker and the kids—Grayson, Presley, and Layla; Dawn O'Leary; Rich Louv; and all the others I've invariably overlooked.

To all my generous friends and sponsors throughout the years, including Gary and Beverly Yamamoto; Gary and Susan Loomis; Toyo Shimano; Ken Sasaki; Larry Evans; Al Perkinson at Costa Del Mar; Scott Leysath; Julie Schuster at Bass Pro Shops; Mark Wilson; and all the gang from the Fred Hall Shows.

To my literary agent, Sammie Justesen, for believing in second chances. To my terrific editor, Kaleena Cote, for her vision and tireless efforts to make this project a reality. Thanks for going to bat for me at every turn. . . .

A special thanks to Ellen Urban and Eileen Clawson for cleaning up the rough edges so beautifully.

And for every dog that has graced my life.

woof

Introduction

We be of one blood, thou and I.

—RUDYARD KIPLING

TIFFANY HAD DECIDED THAT it was time for an adventure. It had been six months since her owners had walked away, and she was ready to run.

It was now or never.

She was the last dog I would have figured for a breakout. She had never caused trouble in the past. She was quiet and extremely well behaved. She was polite on her leash, rarely barked, and always came when called. Little did we know she had been practicing how to open her kennel gate for weeks.

She must have known that the kennel techs were leaving the main door to her barracks partially open at night. She also must have known that the janitor finished cleaning the main building around 7:30 p.m. And that he drove a 1977 Volvo sedan with no muffler. I can only imagine how it all happened. . . .

Around 8:00 on Friday night, she waited until that old car pulled out of the shelter parking lot. Then, she jumped up on her gate, pressed her nose against the bars, and flicked up the latch with her paw. The gate swung open with a triumphant crash against the concrete wall.

She raced down the hall to the barracks door. As usual, it was partially open but not far enough for her to squeeze through. So she pushed. And squeezed. And pushed. And squeezed. Each time, the massive door opened a little more. Finally, there was enough room to squeeze through.

She was free.

For the first time in six months, she felt the cool night air on the tip of her nose. She galloped across the dirt parking lot, jumped over a short chain-link fence into the field next door, and never looked back.

She had forgotten how wonderful the wild grasses felt rushing across her face. About the sound of the wind whistling in her ears. The feeling of her paws bounding on the wild earth, the taste of freedom and a life filled with adventure.

She had forgotten what it was like to be a dog.

She ran for three days and nights, exploring the many backyards in the neighborhood, taking sips from swimming pools, and weaving her way through jungle gyms and swing sets. She even ran with the children for a spell during recess at the local elementary school.

The adventure continued.

Tiffany had always wanted to walk down Main Street off her leash. So she headed for town. She trotted past the bank and the hardware store. She flirted with a handsome standard poodle tied to a No Parking sign next to the post office. She stopped and sniffed a bicycle tire in front of the library. She lingered a bit outside the local market, tempted by the aromas beckoning from behind the automatic sliding-glass doors. A few kind faces tried to approach her, but she kept her distance. Once someone read the blue bone-shaped shelter tag on her collar, her adventure would be over.

Besides, she still had many things to see.

Tiffany turned west and ran through fields dotted with brown-skinned men and women who wore wide-brimmed hats and put tomatoes into wooden bushel baskets. They called to her as she ran down the rows of red and green.

"Perro Blanca! Perro Blanca!"

Their voices sounded sweet in the misty morning air.

At night, she galloped down the long, lush fairways of the public golf course. The soft spray of the water left little droplets on her long whiskers and bathed her dusty coat clean. When she got tired, she'd find a grove of pepper trees and fall asleep beneath their weeping branches to the sounds of crickets in the tall grass.

On the third day she stepped in a gopher hole while running across a soccer field.

It was time to go back.

We found her limping in a church parking lot next door to the shelter. While everyone examined her paw and counted cuts and bruises, I quietly celebrated the sparkle in her eyes—the kind of thing that only comes from going on adventures.

The following stories are just a small tribute to the many dogs that have never failed to bring richness, meaning, and adventure to my life. It is my hope that these pages will inspire you to visit your local shelter, where hundreds of dogs are just waiting to do the same for you.

And when I think of all the wealth, joy, and security they've brought to my life, I have to go way back to the beginning, to the best dog any boy could wish for. A dog named Rusty.

woof

the Power
of Paws

WHEN I WAS A BOY, I was convinced that a ghost lived in my bedroom closet. My parents had renovated the attic of our brown-shingled Dutch Colonial and turned it into two bedrooms: one for me and one for my younger brother, Glenn. His room was on the sunny south side of the house. It was simple, boxy, and bright with two good-size windows and a small closet. It also faced our next-door neighbors' house, a mere thirty feet away. With our best friend Pete's bedroom window directly across from Glenn's room, it was safe and secure, and we often set up elaborate paper-cup gondola and cable-car systems strung high across the driveway, by way of which we traded baseball cards and exchanged homework assignments.

My bedroom, on the north side, had spooky nooks, landings, and sharp-angled ceilings that dipped to darkened corners and creepy crawl spaces. The lone window looked out over Bianchi's Wholesale Greenhouses next door—a maze of spooky glass houses, black tarp-covered bales of peat, and a monstrous brick smokestack that towered over the neighborhood below. My room also hosted the biggest closet in the house. And every night before I went to sleep, that closet door would have to be closed.

Sometimes I would feign bravery and leave the door open a crack. I would boldly turn off the lights, pull the covers up, and close my eyes. I'd call to my brother in the next room for comfort and assurance.

". . . Glenn?"

No answer. He always fell asleep before I did.

Then a rogue creak or mysterious thump would spring my eyes open and set my pulse racing. I would peek over the covers and watch the door like a red-tailed hawk. The hall light would begin to play tricks with my wide eyes and tender imagination, and that small crack of pitch black leading into the closet would begin to grow. The gold doorknob would slowly begin to turn and the tips of ghoulish fingers would appear, curling around the door frame.

"Daaadd! Come close the closet door!" I'd yell.

My dad would bound up the stairs, three steps at a time, and close the door for me. With a smile, he would assure me that the ghost was not strong enough to open the door by himself. I don't think he ever tried to convince me that the ghost wasn't there. He'd just always come to the rescue.

One Tuesday morning when I was very young, an incredibly thin, baked-potato-brown dog appeared on our front steps.

"I opened the door and this little dog was just standing there," my mother recalls. "He was an absolute mess."

Not quite sure what to do, she called my father, who immediately came home and took him to see our vet, Dr. Barry. It turned out that our unexpected guest had one of the worst cases of mange he had ever seen. Nobody at the animal hospital thought he was going to make it. "I'll try my best to save him," he told us. "But it's very serious."

A week later, after a series of intense treatments with arsenic—the only remedy for such advanced cases of mange at the time—he started to turn the corner.

My mother said it was a miracle that he recovered. Slowly he regained his strength. And all those bare patches of skin and brown mats of fur were soon replaced with as glorious an orange coat as I'd ever seen.

We named him Rusty. And he would become the dog against which I would measure all others.

To this day my mother says there will never be another dog like him. And though my memories of him are fuzzy and gilded by a simpler and more innocent time, an imprint on my heart says it's so, too.

With the passing of years, I have forgotten many of the details about Rusty. Most have dissolved into myth or are bound by stories shared at dinner tables and in holiday living rooms. I look at old photographs: I see a dog sitting beside me on a braided rug in front of a small Christmas tree. I want to remember the touch of his fur. I see a young boy sitting proudly on a blue Schwinn bicycle with a dog standing beside him. I want to remember the sound of his bark. I see two brothers hugging and wrestling with a dog on the front lawn. I want to remember everything about him.

But I can't. Too much time has passed.

A SHEPHERD/COLLIE MIX, RUSTY was as stately, handsome, and heroic as any dog I have ever known. His rich coat was indeed golden orange, except for the fantastic white blaze that ran down his sturdy chest and the snowy splash at the tip of his magnificent tail. He was my protector, my friend, my confidant, and my hero. Fiercely loyal, he would do battle with any dog that dared cross the line of our property, and while he was serious and very task oriented, he never turned down an offer for a good wrestle or roughhouse session on our front lawn.

"He loves you boys more than anything," my mother often said.

He never got sick. Occasionally he would come home a bit banged up after a fight with his neighborhood rival, a street-tough little mutt named Frankie. But he always recovered quickly, and after a few days' rest he would be back outside making sure our yard was a safe place for my brother and me to have a catch.

Rusty

However, Rusty didn't appreciate being asked to do dog tricks. Every now and then he would begrudgingly shake your hand if you pestered him long enough.

Kisses? Never.

My dad did dress him up once as the disguised wolf from Little Red Riding Hood. Complete with a headscarf and cape, he valiantly obliged for one snapshot. I never told him it made the local paper.

He was quite cooperative when it came to sitting and posing for the yearly black-and-white Christmas cards my parents had done for the better part of my childhood, always responding to the urgings and attention-grabbing whistles of the professional photographer behind the big 8-by-10 camera and striking poses that would make Rin Tin Tin proud.

If he had one bad habit, it was that he loved to chase cars. But after one particular close call, I screamed and yelled and begged him to stop; I told him I didn't want to see him die. I was eight years old. He never did it again.

He would regularly disappear, sometimes for as long as three days. Mom would worry and fret. Dad would joke that he was just visiting all his girlfriends. Then out of the blue he would show up at the bus stop, greet my brother and me with a smile and a tail wag or two, and escort us home. We never did find out where he went.

Rusty was also our constant companion on our trips to the local delicatessen, trotting faithfully beside our bicycles after a neighborhood football game or hockey match. He'd then patiently sit beside us on the concrete steps as we gulped down bottles of orange soda and root beer, always hoping for a piece of a roast beef sandwich or a spare greasy potato chip. He was our personal chaperone and mascot, an immeasurable part of our "neighborhood gang," and we always felt a little bit safer when he was around.

One afternoon, on our way home from a baseball game, he broke up a fight between the neighborhood bully and me, growling and leaping into the fray before things got out of hand. In many ways, he was the big brother I never had, the guardian angel of my childhood who watched over me at all times. I can't imagine any part of my young life without him.

So on those nights when my father would come leaping up the stairs to close the closet door, I would always ask him to do one more thing— call Rusty upstairs to stay with me. Instantly he'd yell, "Rusty! Come here, boy!" Soon, I would hear his generous paws loping up the stairs. He would greet us energetically with a tail wag or two and then dutifully jump up on the end of my bed, heave a hefty sigh, and fall sound asleep. And if the ceilings started playing tricks on me, or if doorknobs started to turn or curtains became ghostly, all I had to do was reach out with my toes and feel the warmth of Rusty's back. That's when I'd know that nothing could ever hurt me in the darkness.

AS TIME PASSED, GIRLFRIENDS, NEW driver's licenses, and college entrance exams replaced our walks home from the bus stop and from afternoon wrestling matches. Rusty was getting older, and so was I. And like so many aspects of my childhood, my memories of his death are as fuzzy as those of his arrival. I remember a phone call to my college dorm. I was homesick and lonely, and my mother and I hadn't been getting along too well. The week before, she'd received a phone call in the middle of the night from the East Orange police department. On a liquor-store run, I had totaled my new car of only three days. I could barely hear her voice because of the party going on next door.

"Gary," she began, "I have some bad news. Rusty died this morning."

Just then, someone knocked on the door and offered me a beer.

"Mom," I said, covering my ears, "it's kind of crazy here. Can I call you back?"

I hung up the phone and rested my head against the concrete wall. It would be another twenty-five years before I would cry the tears that filled my eyes that cold October night.

On the eve of my forty-third birthday, I would call my mother to finish the conversation we had started so many years ago.

"Your father found him lying on the kitchen floor that morning," she told me. "He couldn't get up. We called Dr. Barry, and he told us to bring him over. It all happened so quickly. He had been fine the day before."

I swallowed hard and picked up a photo that I kept on my desk— an eight-year-old boy hugging a perfect dog. I began to remember the sound of his bark.

"Was he in a lot of pain?" I asked.

"If he was, he never let us know. Not a whine. Not a whimper. Your father took him up to the hospital. I couldn't go."

"I understand, Mom. Did you have a chance to say goodbye?"

"Yes," she said. "Because when your father carried him down the front steps that morning, I knew he wasn't coming back home."

I looked at the photo and thought of the many nights Rusty had slept on the end of my bed and kept my feet warm. I began to remember the softness of his fur.

"I guess I never thought he would die," I said.

"I know," my mom said softly. "But when you left for college, I think he knew his job was finished."

"What job?"

As I put the photo back in its place, my mother replied, "Watching over you."

woof

CHAPTER 2

Juliet and Dolores

I GREW UP IN THE ERA of cocktail parties, LPs, and cigarettes. There were no such things as designated drivers, digital downloads, or secondhand smoke. Being the son of a popular local radio disk jockey, I was exposed to more than my share of booze, butts, and Big Bands. But I didn't mind. I loved the fact that most of the adults around me worshipped Frank Sinatra, knew how to make whiskey sours, and collected Chesterfield coupons. I can't imagine a more rich and entertaining way to grow up. And despite my parents' friends' indulgence at times regarding the aforementioned vices, there was always somebody around to give me a swift kick in the ass if I needed one.

Everyone smoked at the radio station—the receptionist, the boss's secretary, the sales staff, the engineers, and all of the disk jockeys save my father (who only occasionally smoked a pipe on weekends). At home, my mother smoked Newports for years, and my grandmother could easily go through three packs of Chesterfields a day. She lived to be eighty-two. Go figure.

I loved to watch my grandmother smoke. It was like watching an artist at work. While sipping her Dewar's old-fashioned in our living room each night, she would begin her performance by carefully setting down her wares on the old cobbler's bench in front of our couch. She always kept her cigarettes in an elegant leather case that had two gold snaps at the top. Her silver lighter was heavy and worn, its edges round and softened from use, and the crystal ashtray she kept in her purse at all times was solid and thick.

I marveled at her ability to carry on a conversation as her long, sophisticated fingers opened the case and gently tapped out the soft-packed rolls of tobacco. Like a concert pianist, she would begin these smoking sonatas never once needing to look down at the keys. She would slowly bring the cigarette to her mouth, never breaking stride in a sentence or thought, raise that magnificent lighter, flip the cap with a clink, and light the flame with a sturdy snap of her thumb. The paper and tobacco would crackle as she drew in her first puff, and the sweet aroma of butane lingered in the air as she closed the cap of her silver-cased torch and set it down on the bench. The first movement of her recital was finished.

Like cigarettes and smoking, when I was growing up, the rules surrounding what our dogs could and couldn't do were much less restrictive. There were no leash laws, and like my friends and me, most dogs were free to wander about the neighborhood. Boundaries and territories were understood and respected, and almost everyone got along. There were places to go and places to stay away from, and we all came home at the end of the day.

It was also a time when a boy's first job was, most likely, a paper route. I was ten years old when I got mine, delivering a weekly newspaper called the *Long Island Advance* on Thursday afternoons after school to twenty-eight houses on my trusty blue Schwinn bicycle. Practically outfitted with dual metal newspaper baskets draped above pinstriped back fenders and a headlight/horn/AM radio that was attached to the handlebars, it was nowhere near as fast or as fashionable as George Van Schaick's three-speed English Racer (sans rear fender, of course, for the "coolness" effect), but it got the job done. And though I begged for one just like his, my family was very traditional when it came to such things, rarely caving in to peer pressure regarding my desires for the latest fads in bikes, toys, or clothing.

Just a few houses up from ours, where one of my newpaper customers lived, was also home to one of the neighborhood's biggest troublemakers—the aforementioned street-tough little mutt named Frankie—who'd routinely test the boundaries of our front yard, much to the irritation of my dog, Rusty. While I was delivering papers, he paid me little mind, sometimes even coming up to say hello. But the moment he showed up at our house and start sniffing around the wagon wheels framing the entrance to our driveway, it was game on—Rusty would come charging across the lawn to do battle with his arch rival. Their encounters were more scuffles than fights, and the decade-long quarrel didn't end until Frankie got too old and stiff to make the trek down to our house.

Other than a charge by a Doberman that escaped from its yard one time, only to be called back quickly into the house by its owner just before it got to me, my two-mile route was relatively free of dog drama. Still, I was always on the lookout for that one bad experience our postman always talked about.

"Damn German shepherd over on Hedges Road," he'd say. "Only one that ever got me."

Less than one month into my new route, I met my Waterloo, courtesy of an extremely large German shepherd. Apparently, his owners had decided to move from Hedges Road to the end of Roosevelt Boulevard.

I'd just signed up the family, and their house was in a fairly remote location, not far from the deserted barge where I used to fish with my family on Great South Bay. On their first delivery date, right as I was carefully putting the folded-up newspaper into their brand new plastic mailbox, a German shepherd guard dog, fresh off the set of *Hogan's Heroes,* leapt off the front porch and started running, full tilt, straight toward me. I have long since learned that it's the quiet ones you need to be extra careful about—and this dog was silent and focused. I was certain that the next time he'd open his mouth would be to take a chunk out of my leg.

I ran up to the side of my bicycle, snapped up the kickstand, and started to run, urging its fat tires forward with a few well-planted hops and skips in preparation for jumping onboard. Just as I was about to throw my right leg over the seat, the shepherd grabbed hold of my left pant leg that I'd just anchored to the rubber bike pedal on the left side. I yelled and kicked and screamed at him, all the while trying to build up a little speed on my navy blue slug on two wheels. He finally let go but continued to give chase down the dead-end road, growling each time he got closer, until he finally peeled off about a quarter mile from his house. Needless to say, that afternoon, sans approval from corporate headquarters, I personally cancelled that family's subscription and never ventured down Roosevelt Boulevard again.

I did get to meet an assortment of small housedogs on my route—pugs, dachshunds, and Boston terriers—cute little yappers and barkers that always put up a fuss from behind front screen doors when I'd try to collect my 25 cents for the paper. It was the only time in my young life that I had any contact with anything that even resembled a small dog.

Except for Juliet.

In many families, well-defined allegiances often develop between family members and pets. Throughout the years, the relationships in our home have been clear: Canyon and Squeeze were my dogs. Brody was my wife Linda's dog and presently, both Linda and my daughter, Hayden, share our fox terrier Cielo's affections, with me coming in a distant third. Although these alliances may blur at times—especially if there's an accident that needs to be cleaned up on the living-room carpet ("Look what *your* dog did!")—there is no doubt that the next time a thunderstorm rolls around, Cielo will be curled up in Linda's lap and my latest devotee, Smokey, will be sitting on my head.

When I was a boy, Rusty was my dog. And there was no question that Juliet was my mother's dog.

Back then, there was also little pressure to have dogs spayed or neutered. Like my friends and me, most dogs were free to wander about the neighborhood. Boundaries and territories were understood and respected, and almost everyone got along. We spent more time outdoors than indoors and every evening, just has the sun was going down, you'd hear a chorus of callings from front doors and porches up and down our block, beckoning both children and faithful pups to come home for dinner. Whether you were a kid or a dog, it was a time when we all lived life on looser reins.

As a result, both of our dogs, my perfect dog, Rusty, and his female companion, Juliet, had full reproductive capabilities. Subsequently, my mother and father faced a unique set of challenges whenever Juliet "came into season." The reason? Rusty was a seventy-five-pound shepherd/collie mix, and Juliet was a fifteen-pound dachshund.

And quite the amorous couple they were! Despite their immense size differences, according to my mom, they couldn't keep their paws off each other. More than once she'd have to drag out the garden hose and hose them down in the backyard, making sure that Rusty would back off. "I was always afraid she might suffocate!" my mother exclaimed.

Another time, the two dogs got so locked up together that my mother had to call our vet. I had heard of such things but always thought it was the stuff of pet lore and urban legend. But she swore this really happened. "It took Dr. Barry about twenty minutes to separate them," she added.

Now that's a visual I'd like to file in the same drawer as the one of my father pulling a pair of my mother's pantyhose out of the backside of our golden retriever, Honey, one winter morning—an item, in true golden retriever form, that Honey had decided to eat the night before.

Unfortunately, as a result of that final, passionate lockup, Juliet got pregnant. On the advice of Dr. Barry, it was decided to abort the pregnancy. Later my mom said this was because of their extraordinary difference in size; Juliet would never have survived birthing the puppies.

A few months later, my parents decided to mate Juliet with something a little more in her ballpark—a miniature dachshund. Their friend and coworker at the radio station, the irascible Phil Roll, who also owned a female dachshund named Dolores, referred the stud to them. The result was an adorable, single black male puppy that was born in the hall closet next to their bedroom—just as they were walking out the door for dinner.

Once again, Dr. Barry came to the rescue.

It was a very difficult birth. Juliet was howling and screaming in the back of the closet and wouldn't come out. And there, hunched down on the floor, was Dr. Barry—his hands and knees in the hallway, his body halfway inside the closet—delivering the puppy. Now *that's* what I call a house call.

A GIFT FROM OUR NEXT-DOOR neighbors, Emil and Delphine, for most of my childhood Juliet was almost invisible to me. I loved Rusty so much that I paid her little attention. What I didn't know was how much Rusty loved her.

Whenever my brother and I would be at school, my mom said the two of them were inseparable. Juliet followed Rusty everywhere. And Rusty was always very kind and protective of Juliet, especially when any other dogs came on the property. "But the moment you came home, she'd quietly surrender his attentions back to you and your brother and retreat to her favorite living-room chair and fall asleep, usually belly to belly with Sweet Kitty," my mother remembered.

I thought of Juliet the same way as I did Sweet Kitty, our very devoted and mild-mannered house cat. They were always there, but I was too busy doing boy things to notice. Only now can I appreciate how important they were in taming the fabric and atmosphere of our household. They were a steady and reliable presence in our often chaotic and unpredictable home.

Sadly, one day Juliet's devotion and attachment to Rusty led to her getting hit by a car in front of our house. Lacking the street smarts and outdoor awareness that Rusty had, she lagged behind him one day while crossing the road. My mother watched the whole thing happen. The man who hit her didn't even stop; She never had a chance.

Not long after Juliet died, my father's annual company Christmas party was held at the bay-front home of one of the more flamboyant employees of the radio station. Never known for humility or under-statement, Phil Roll, WALK's one-of-a-kind traffic and program man-ager, would spend weeks personally preparing the holiday feast for the entire staff—a gourmet spread worthy of inclusion in any food or culinary magazine. He would go to all this trouble despite the fact most of his coworkers couldn't stand him.

Regardless of the fact that he was a royal, arrogant pain in the ass 90 percent of the time, my family still loved him. He was an inimitable, flagrant presence in our lives—a perfect part-time addition to our crazy and fun-loving family.

"I firmly believe that your mother and Phil Roll were separated at birth," my mom often said to my father. With both my grandmothers' and Phil's affinity for Chesterfields and Scotch, she might have been right.

Invariably, Phil would call my mom the morning of the party, on the verge of hysterics because he'd run out of balsamic vinegar or fresh parsley. When my mom would suggest a possible substitute for the missing ingredients, Phil would hear nothing of it.

"Dorothy, darling, we might as well all go to McDonalds!" he'd snap when she suggested he use almonds instead of pine nuts for his pesto dish.

Phil also refused to serve beer at any of his parties.

"For the peasants and commoners," he'd retort.

No, his wet bar was top-shelf only, where manhattans, vodka martinis ("shaken, not stirred," of course) and fifty-year-old cognac held court. And if you happened to order an old-fashioned, know it was going to be Dewar's or Chivas Scotch only.

Juliet

Back in those days, it was my job to park and retrieve cars at holiday parties. (How anyone made it back home alive back then is beyond me.) It was always my mom and dad who were the last to leave, with my mom always helping with the dishes and cleanup. That night was no different.

"It was a lovely meal, Phil," my mom said while wiping down the dining-room table.

"The Black Truffle Soufflé was a total disaster," he wailed. "I told Randy that he needed to beat the egg whites longer, but, as usual, he totally ignored me."

Randy, Phil's housemate, overhearing Phil's criticism from the living room, stormed into the kitchen. He was holding Dolores, Phil's three-year-old dachshund, under his arm.

"You've done nothing but nag and bitch at me all night long, and I've had it!" he yelled.

He then pulled open the sliding-glass doors, walked outside, ran to the water's edge, and promptly threw Dolores into the bay.

"Dolores!" Phil screamed, throwing the soufflé dish high into the air.

In a complete panic, Phil tore off his plaid apron, and ran blindly through the open back door. "Dolores! My Dolores!" he continued to wail as he awkwardly stumbled across the sand.

Fortunately, there was a full moon that night, so Phil was able to spot her right away. But she had taken in quite a bit of water, and by the time he actually reached her, she was having trouble breathing.

To this day, my father still has a hard time believing what he saw next.

With a soaking wet, freezing wiener dog cradled in his arms, Phil raced back into the house. And in between cursing Randy for what he'd done and placing a choking and gurgling Dolores on the white shag carpet in the dining room, Phil started doing what any responsible and loving pet owner would do. Well, maybe.

He started giving Dolores mouth-to-mouth resuscitation.

"I thought your father was going to lose his Black Truffle Soufflé on the spot," my mom said.

Whether or not Phil's course of action made a difference or not in Dolores's survival is debatable. She did, however, completely recover from the ordeal and bore no permanent effects from the incident. I'm not sure I can say the same for my father.

"Once you see a grown man give mouth to mouth to a dachshund, you never quite look at him the same way again," my father said.

I'll drink to that.

woof

CHAPTER 3

Sable Sue

I HAVE THIS RECURRING DREAM in which I'm standing in my high school locker room after having just finished gym class. It's the last day of school. Everyone is cleaning out lockers, showering, getting dressed, laughing, joking, and ultimately leaving. Except for me.

I sit down on a damp, wooden bench in front of a bank of gray lockers. I can't remember which one is mine, but I know it's in this general area. I think there are some things inside my locker that I don't want to leave behind, but I'm not sure. Fortunately, only a couple of lockers have locks on them, so finding mine shouldn't be too difficult. There's only one problem—I don't know the right combination. By this time, everyone is gone, and I'm alone. No matter how hard I try, I can't figure out the right combination.

Calling Dr. Freud.

I would like to believe that there is a perfect home for every dog in the world, that the right combination is always just a moment away. During my tenure at the shelter, I never gave up hope, even for the most desperate dogs. That being said, there were always a few for whom I didn't think we would ever find the right combination. But time and time again, I watched as tiny miracles took place every day.

Sable Sue

For Nike, a frantic young German shepherd pup who was terrified of children, we found the right combination in a childless young couple that understood the time, attention, and patience he needed.

I had all but given up on Puppy Girl, a wild-eyed black shepherd/retriever mix who spent most of her time in her kennel spinning, barking, and charging the bars. But one afternoon, we found the right combination for her in a quiet, middle-aged man who said she reminded him of his childhood dog.

Then there was Newton—the 130-pound lovable, slobbering goliath of a bloodhound whose favorite pastime was knocking people over. We found the perfect combination in a big ex-football player who was strong enough to handle him yet patient enough to give him the training he needed.

Jeter was found running with a pack of strays on Long Island. Filthy and covered with ticks, he was one of the wildest and most unapproachable dogs ever to pass through an animal shelter's doors. That was until he fell in love with Christa, my five-year-old niece, who unlocked the combination to his wild heart.

I was convinced that Patches was part wolf or coyote. Aside from the obvious physical similarities, there was something in her eyes—a wild and wary aura that seemed to guide and temper her every move. I wanted to connect with her. But she wouldn't let me.

On our first meeting, she walked to the farthest corner of her kennel, turned around, sat down facing the wall, and totally ignored me. On our twentieth meeting, she walked to the farthest corner of her kennel, turned around, sat down facing the wall, and totally ignored me. On our fiftieth meeting, she walked to the farthest corner of her kennel, turned around, sat down facing the wall, yawned, and *then* totally ignored me.

"Ah, now we're getting somewhere," I mumbled sarcastically.

There was only one person that was allowed to get near her, my good friend Jane, who was one of the most intuitive kennel techs at the shelter. She was also part Cherokee.

Understanding the Native American culture's deep connection with both the wolf and the coyote, I had a feeling that Jane was the only hope for Patches. And I was right. Jane eventually took Patches home—the right combination.

And everyone loved Butch, a bashful Snickers bar of a border collie mix, who would roll over on his back and pee on anyone that approached him. After a long (and damp) courtship, I found the right combination in a shy young girl around whom Butch felt perfectly safe and comfortable.

Others, I worried about. Pooh-Bear and Bandita. Tara and Socks. Brandon and Jeter. And Cody.

I was deeply concerned about Cody right from the start. I had never seen a dog so desperate to get out of his kennel. Surrendered as a four-year-old untrained, unneutered, and underloved black Lab, Cody was a slobbering, leaping mess of fear and panic. I couldn't imagine how anyone passing by his kennel would consider him for adoption. Yet I knew that beneath all that craziness was a wonderful dog. I could see it in his kind eyes.

So he became another one of my projects. I would take temporary custody—be his interim foster parent, his accomplice to freedom.

Armed with a roll of paper towels, for three months I went to see him first thing in the morning. He would pant and slobber so much during the night that his entire neck and chest would become soaking wet. I would dry him off, talk to him softly, and try my best to calm him down. I usually left his kennel full of hair, slobber, and scratch marks from paws not wanting me to leave.

After I cleaned him up, we'd go for a walk out to the playfield. Beyond happy to be outside, he'd trot along beside me with a big smile on his face, never pulling on his leash, perfectly content to stay right by my side. Once we reached the open field, he would lift his nose high into the air and breathe in all the scents sailing on the breeze.

He was very methodical when it came to taking care of his business. He chose his spots carefully, and when he was finished he would rake his front and back claws across the ground like a bull preparing to charge a phantom matador. If it was an attempt to cover up what he had just deposited, he never came close.

He was black as coal, a little chubby but strong. His dark brown eyes were always filled with hope and eagerness, and when he wagged his tail, the entire rear quarter of his body swayed from side to side like an eighteen-wheeler caught in a stiff crosswind.

He was also a major leaner. If I stopped to have a conversation with someone on our way to the playfield, before I knew it he'd be leaning against my leg. If I sat on a bench, he would come over, sit down, and lean against my knee. When I took him to schools as part of the outreach program, he would lean against my shoulder as I drove. I love it when dogs lean on me. God knows I've leaned on my share throughout the years.

With the thought of leaving him in his kennel just too much to bear, I brought him inside my office every day. He was most content lying on top of my feet under my desk. This way he knew I couldn't leave without his knowing. It was the only time I ever saw him close his eyes and rest. I tried to keep my feet very still, knowing of his many sleepless nights.

One afternoon, while working at my desk, a man poked his head around my office door and asked me where the restrooms were.

"Around the corner to your left," I replied.

"Thanks! By the way, who is that?" he asked, pointing toward my feet.

"Oh, that's Cody. He can't handle being in the kennel all alone so I keep him up here with me during the day."

"Is he up for adoption?"

"He sure is," I said with a smile.

Two days later, Cody had a new pair of feet to sleep on.

MY OFFICIAL TITLE AT THE center was "humane educator." My job was to teach middle school students about pet care, responsibility, and the humane treatment of animals. Over time, I discovered that the students took care of the dogs and cats just fine—it was the humane treatment of *each other* that they needed to work on.

It was a ten-week summer program, and each week I taught a different group of twenty to twenty-five kids. I was constantly trying to find the most effective ways to reach them, my goal being that once the week was over, they would be young and fervent ambassadors for the many Codys of the world. I realized early on that the dogs, not I, would teach them the most important lessons.

Every Monday, I had the students "adopt" dogs for the week. The first few days they would sit outside their dogs' kennels and talk, observe, and get to know them. Toward the middle of the week, with the generous help of the kennel techs, they'd actually get to meet, play, and have their pictures taken with their dogs.

Jeter

As one might expect, most students were drawn to the most outgoing and cutest dogs—the retrievers, the terriers, and the puppies. But one outsider, a tough little kid named Tim, picked Sable Sue right away.

Sable had been at the shelter for almost three years, a longer stint than any of the other dogs. As fragile and frightened as any dog I have ever known, Sable Sue was a boxer mix with a gentle face and forever-troubled eyes. There was almost a constant tremble in her thin body, and even the slightest bump or noise would send her flying into a corner. She panted incessantly, always trying to catch her breath in a world full of too many surprises, too many unknowns.

I sat with her often. It's hard to sit with a dog that has known only bars and cement walls most of its life. The walls are high, like huge concrete blinders to the world outside. In the solitude of her kennel, Sable spent many hours looking for and fearing things she would never see.

I wondered if there would be a tiny miracle in her life.

Bright, witty, and tough-minded, Sable's suitor, Tim, had been anointed by his male classmates to be their prepubescent king. The

Clown King—king of laughs, king of the tightrope he would walk many times with me. And as any eleven-year-old boy feeling his oats might do, he graciously accepted his coronation immediately.

When I first meet a dog in the kennels, I do not judge it on its initial bark or cower. I often stand sturdy and silent, just to let it know that, at the very least, I'm curious about its behavior. I did the same with Tim. That first day, he lobbed a couple of wisecracks at me, to the nervous delight of his followers. I looked at him firmly, just to let him know that I was aware of the shots he'd fired across my bow, but I said nothing. Some kids like to test boundaries more than others. Usually there's a reason.

I noticed something change in Tim when he sat with Sable. His face softened, and tenderness awakened. He spoke in respectful tones. When I felt the moment was right, I'd walk over and sit beside him, and we'd talk about her pretty coat and her sad eyes. I'd explain to him that some dogs were stronger than others, some were weaker, and that often there was a leader—an alpha male, a dog that all the others respected and looked up to. I told Tim he was one of the stronger ones.

Like so many dogs before her, Sable had become our bridge.

In the classroom, Tim was still testing me. One afternoon, I was preparing to give an exam. At Tim's age, sexual innuendo is at a premium, so when I mentioned that anyone caught looking at another student's test papers would be "penalized," I saw Tim's Round Table band of knights look to him in eager anticipation of a wise-ass remark. He looked up at me and then back down at his exam and quietly wrote his name on the top of the sheet. I turned and walked triumphantly back toward my desk thinking that Tim and I had turned a corner. Then a low mutter came from the back of the classroom, followed by a smattering of chuckles. I turned around and looked at Tim. He had a mischievous smile on his face.

Progress, not perfection.

On Fridays the students wrote letters to the dogs they had adopted for the week and then read them to the class. Their letters were remarkable testimonies to the inherent sensitivity that children have toward animals. To hear words like "I love you with all my heart" over and over again makes me believe that the future for dogs like Sable Sue is in good hands. It also tells me that dogs are invaluable partners in helping us to discover or rediscover a place where we can love with "all our hearts."

Tim was the last student to read his letter. His entourage was restless and wired, anxious to roll and tumble out of their seats in laughter at Tim's first utterance. He walked up to the front of the class and began:

> Dear Sable,
> I know what it's like to live in an orphanage. I used to be an orphan without a home. If I can get adopted, I know you can, too.
> With all my heart, Tim

Tiny miracles.

woof

CHAPTER 4

Waldo

FOR MANY OF US, THERE is one special summer that towers above the rest. A summer so wonderful, so full of carefree memories and good times, that it's almost too painful to look back on. A summer of untethered freedom and joyful irresponsibility, where days flowed seamlessly into each other and nights were forgiving and full of promise and wonder. For my last great summer, I worked as a bellhop and lifeguard at Gurney's Inn, a very popular beachfront resort and spa just west of Montauk, on the easternmost tip of Long Island, New York. It was the best summer job one could ask for, where a pocketful of dollar-bill tips could last for days and a quarter tank of gas would get you anywhere you needed to go. This was my "last hurrah," so to speak, before I entered into the "real world."

I secured a beach house with a crew that included my younger brother Glenn, our best friend and long-time next-door neighbor Pete, a couple of childhood pals, and a relatively new friend named Ted, who was also an investment banker on Wall Street. By using Ted's work credentials and assurances to the realtor that they'd never find better tenants, we managed to charm our way into an affordable three-bedroom ranch about a mile from the beach. Like many first-time house-sharing ventures, that summer had disaster written all over it. But despite the fact

Waldo

that we were so blind and naive as to the challenges and responsibilities of sharing a house together, we all had one thing in common.

We were surfers.

There's hardly a more dedicated or close-knit family than the brothers and sisters whose lives revolve around weather reports, Sex Wax, and catching the perfect wave. We were no different. Surfing was the glue that held us all together, and there wasn't any dispute, argument, or hangover that couldn't be mended or diffused by a session in the water together.

Of course, no surf house was complete without its very own "wave dog" either. Ours was called Waldo.

What's a wave or surf dog? It's the dog you see while on vacation, waiting patiently in the back of an old pickup truck outside a market or liquor store (sans leash, of course) while the owner is inside getting a sandwich or picking up a six-pack of beer. It's the dog that everybody knows at the most popular surfing spot, the dog that always gets the last bite of an Egg McMuffin or breakfast burrito. It's the dog that is content to just hang out on the beach while you surf for five hours, maybe wandering around a bit, respectfully accepting the attention of kids building sandcastles or parents offering free handouts of pretzels or crackers. It's the dog that never judges your less-than-sterling choices regarding women or alcohol on summer Saturday nights and will even stick beside you as you quote passages from Kahlil Gibran to nice Midwestern girls you just met a few hours earlier on the beach. It wouldn't be a stretch to say that wave dogs are the coolest dogs on earth.

When it came to surf dogs in Montauk, most of the locals had your basic Heinz 57 mixed-breed mutts with an occasional black or yellow Lab thrown into the bunch. So when we showed up that first day at our favorite surf break with Waldo tagging along behind, I'm sure most of the locals in the water figured that a film crew from New York was scouting locations to shoot an upcoming sequel to *The Shaggy Dog*. The star? Why, Waldo, our very own Old English sheepdog, who, for the next three months, would become the official wave dog for the best summer of our lives.

To say that Waldo stuck out like a sore thumb on the beach would be an understatement of the highest order. Tipping the scales at ninety-plus pounds with an endearing bearish gait and a snowy white veil covering his sweet eyes, he looked like he'd taken a wrong turn in the middle of town, bearing right when he should have stayed left, which would have led him to his proper destination: the local Irish pub.

Still, Waldo tried his best to fit in, bounding about in the sand and constantly greeting children and adults alike with his signature nonstop butt-wiggle. The beach was a significant leap for this big, lovable fellow from the fairly constricted confines of his Upper East Side New York City apartment, where he lived with our housemate, Ted. But he never lacked enthusiasm for trying something new, whether it was retrieving balls in the surf or simply chasing seagulls along the shoreline. And he was always up for a breezy ride in our CJ-5 surf jeep.

On weeks when Ted was out of town on business, I'd stay in the city and take care of Waldo. With a spacious apartment that was only a few blocks away from Central Park, it was an easy responsibility—besides, there was no better way to meet girls in Manhattan than by leashing up my woolly bear of a dog for a late-afternoon walk. With this living, breathing conversation piece at my side, I could barely make it a block without being stopped. Waldo dutifully played the charming, oversize puppy, to the delight of his many admirers. He never tired of the attention, and though I never actually got a date as a result of one of our many encounters, it sure was fun to see people's faces light up as he lumbered toward them on the sidewalk.

Once in the park, on the running track just beneath the reservoir at Eighty-sixth Street, I'd let him off the leash to wander around a bit, a mild infraction of a fairly flexible leash law at the time, something that most dog owners broke at least once in a while. Of course, Waldo, in all his resplendent goofiness, would head for the nearest police car, where he'd hunch down by the front bumper and, like a quarterback lining up under center, strategically deposit a ridiculously large mound of business in full view of the attending officers, who were usually trying to enjoy a late-afternoon sandwich or cup of coffee.

As if that weren't enough, apparently having obvious authority-figure issues, he'd then circle the patrol car, lift his leg, and leave his considerable signature on one of the tires. While pulling his leash out of my pocket, I'd just throw up my arms in apology and disbelief—much to the good-natured smiles of the officers—and clean up the mess, scolding Waldo for his impeccable timing and placement. Of course, he had no idea what he had done wrong, and it was impossible to stay angry at his smiling, slobbering face for too long.

And boy, could he slobber! Trips in Ted's open jeep from Manhattan to Montauk on humid, summer Friday afternoons would reduce Waldo to a salivating mess of excitement and anticipation. As hard as we tried to keep him in the back, he'd constantly wiggle his way between the two front seats, turning our 120-mile trip into a windswept droolathon that usually soaked the shoulders of our T-shirts clean through.

With his trademark blue bandana draped around his neck and his ample coat of fur blowing in the breeze, Waldo's happy face exemplified the great weekend escape from the city and with cars whizzing by us on the Long Island Expressway, he'd sit tall beneath the roll bar and slobber away, occasionally acknowledging a honk or two from station wagons and SUVs loaded with coolers, beach chairs and skylines fading away in rearview mirrors. Once we were on the two-lane road through the Hamptons, he'd settle down enough to take a drink or two from his water bowl on the back seat, only to deposit half of his refreshment in my lap while attempting to lick my cheek as we paused at a traffic light. He was a big, lovable clown of a dog, adored by everyone and appreciated by nobody more than me.

Once in Montauk, Waldo was not the savviest or most graceful fellow when it came to the outdoors. He barely had a lick of common sense, and more than once I'd have to rescue him from a steep beach bluff that he'd boldly raced up and was totally clueless, once he reached the top, as to how to get back down.

"I thought you were bred to herd mountain goats," I'd say while cradling his trembling body in my arms, with him slobbering all over me the entire way down.

One afternoon upon returning from the beach, a day in which we'd all left early for a surfing session and had decided to leave Waldo at home, I pulled into the driveway to find him walking around the yard with a red, white, and blue basketball in his mouth. With his sight completely obscured by the large, round object, I watched in disbelief as he ran right past me and slammed into the side of my open car door. As I tried to chase him down, the only thing I could figure was that while attempting to retrieve the regulation-size basketball from the bushes, he'd punctured the item in question with both his upper and lower teeth simultaneously, creating a "finger in the dike" situation.

As a result, no air could escape and he was left with a fully extended jaw, the inability to see where he was going, and the problem of having a very large basketball lodged in his mouth. By the time I got home, he was in full panic mode, and I realized that not only was he totally disoriented, but he was also in a considerable amount of pain. God knows how long he'd been running around bumping into things with his jaw stretched to the breaking point.

I quickly ran into the house, looking for something sharp enough to puncture the tough leather hide and settled on a steak knife. When I finally collared Waldo and calmed him down enough to sit still, I couldn't help but think back to my dog Brodie's full-facial encounter with a porcupine. While Waldo's predicament was not as daunting as my trying to remove fifty reverse-barbed quills from a dog's face in the middle of nowhere, I still had my hands full.

The problem was that with Waldo's jaw being fully extended, the slightest increase in pressure to open his mouth would cause him to cry out in pain. Being alone, I had nobody to hold him, so my only option was to sit on the ice cooler on the front lawn and hold the ball attached to Waldo's mouth between my knees as firmly and as still as possible while holding onto Waldo's collar with my left hand. This way, my right hand would be free to puncture the basketball.

If anyone had pulled up behind us in the driveway that afternoon, they would have immediately thought that they'd stumbled onto the set of *Fargo II*. Between his yelps of pain and my frantic attempts to puncture the basketball with a rapidly dulling steak knife, the fact that my back was turned to any potential visitor would have convinced even the most forgiving mailman or UPS guy that I was trying to kill something.

Finally, after repeated thrusts and slashing, I managed to stab a hole through the leather, setting both air and Waldo's mouth free. He shook his head in relief and thanked me with his familiar big, slobbery kiss.

"You are a total clown," I said, while scouting for any other oversized round objects in the yard. "A total, slobbering clown."

While Waldo approached most things in life with fearless abandon, there was one natural phenomenon that absolutely terrified him:

thunderstorms. When it comes to thunderstorms and dogs, there are probably as many different reactions as there are breeds. Some handle them just fine. Others, like my mom's golden retriever, Goldie, had to be put on tranquilizers if the weather forecast even mentioned the possibility of a thundershower. I've never quite understood a dog's fear of something that occurs so naturally. One would think that they'd be genetically preprogrammed to handle such things, especially when some of my most thunder-fearing dogs would take on a grizzly bear if given the chance.

On one such occasion, I was awakened about 2:00 a.m. by a strange, hot wind blowing from the north accompanied by an almost strobelike series of blindingly bright lightning flashes that seemed to appear out of nowhere. What made this unusual weather even more eerie was that there was barely a clap of thunder to be heard anywhere. I'd heard locals talk about "dry lightning" storms rolling across the east end every now and then, but this was a first for me. Whatever it was, the combination of the warm and devilish winds coupled with the unyielding bursts of light with no echoing thunder made for a very creepy evening, and I cursed the fact that I'd opened every window earlier that day to air out the house.

Since Waldo and I had driven out to Montauk a day early, we were all alone in the haunted house that night, a decision made all the more spooky by the prickly feeling of electricity and uncertainty in the air. The few distant rumbles of thunder had already set Waldo's salivary glands into overdrive, and he followed me around the house like a teething infant while I closed windows.

Curtains flapped and flailed at 90-degree angles, and window blinds rattled angrily in the phantom winds, while the white-hot flashes of lightning transformed even the most benign objects into elements of horror; hence, surfboards resting against walls were now open coffins, and photos of deceased family members were coming alive in picture frames resting on jagged fireplace mantels.

With only two rooms left to go, my slobbering sidekick and I headed back down the hallway toward the bedroom. As we approached the darkened intersection between the doorways to the spare bedroom on the right and the main bathroom on the left, a vicious crosswind blew through the house, causing the bathroom door to slam shut with a sound and force usually reserved for cannons and heavy artillery. Waldo, in an amazing display of nimbleness and agility, shot straight up in the air, as if jettisoned from a spring-loaded trampoline, and landed—all ninety pounds of him—in my arms, like a baby just thrown out of a burning three-story window.

I had all but jumped out of my own skin when that door slammed. But the ridiculous sight of a big, drooling bear of a dog cradled in my arms reduced me to knee-buckling laughter, and we collapsed to the hallway floor in a heap. Realizing that any danger had passed, Waldo started licking my face with the broadest of strokes, my half-hearted protests only adding to his enthusiasm. When I finally pushed him away, I noticed that both the lightning and wind had disappeared as quickly as they had arisen.

I leaned my head against the wall and closed my eyes, pleased to feel the familiar southwest breezes of summer that had quietly returned, gently blowing through windows we hadn't quite reached.

"Surf might be good tomorrow," I said to Waldo. "Really good."

And like every great surf dog, Waldo would be right there with me.

woof

CHAPTER 5

$\mathcal{S}$queeze

TWO YEARS AFTER MY LAST great summer in Montauk, I got married. My new bride, Linda, a San Diego native, had also fallen in love with the east end of Long Island, and we decided to hold our small, mostly family-attended marriage ceremony in a beautiful white Presbyterian church on Main Street in East Hampton. It was a perfect spring day in May.

We chose to have the wedding reception at my old stomping grounds and former workplace, Gurney's Inn, which was only half an hour east of the church. There's something quite redeeming about being on the other side of a table where you'd once obediently cleared dishes and served German chocolate cake to bossy patrons on summer vacations. Besides, the management of the inn gave me a really good package deal on a wedding cake, their seafood appetizer bar, and prime rib dinner entrée.

As an alternative to a honeymoon cruise or vacation, we rented a small weekend cottage for the summer near Ditch Plains Beach, a few miles from the center of Montauk's charming seaside village. On our way back to the cottage from the reception on the old beach highway, the muffler fell off my grandmother's 1967 Ford Fairlane, which we'd chosen to use as a funky alternative to traveling by limo. I can still see

35

Linda standing in the middle of that greasy Texaco garage in her white wedding dress as a couple of mechanics did their best to fix the problem. Once back on the road, and after changing into more casual clothing, we headed down to the docks to grab a late-night snack and a couple of beers. While sampling a platter of fresh clams on the half shell, Linda promptly cracked one of her molars on a rogue piece of shell.

"I hope this isn't a precursor of things to come," she said, while feeling around the back of her mouth with her finger. Luckily, it wasn't. This year, we celebrated our twenty-fifth wedding anniversary.

Toward the end of that first summer together, Linda and I starting talking about adding a dog to our family. Since we'd be spending most of our time in the city, Linda strongly lobbied for a small dog. It would be years before I would come to appreciate or even consider having a dog that was lighter than fifty pounds. I wasn't very open to the idea.

"A medium-sized dog, maybe . . ." I said reluctantly.

On a trip to the local supermarket in Montauk, we saw a sign tacked to the bulletin board in front of the store: FREE TO GOOD HOME. SIX HUSKY/LAB–MIX PUPPIES. CAN VIEW AT MONTAUK MARINE BASIN.

"Want to go take a look?" I asked.

"Sure," Linda replied.

A word to the wise—if you're not serious about getting a dog, you better not take a trip to see six puppies. Odds are that you're going to go home with something furry in your lap. Such was the case with our ride down to the marina. Problem was, we left with the wrong one.

Home to some of the biggest shark tournaments in the country, the Montauk Marine Basin was a short drive from our cottage. When we arrived we were directed by a couple of fishermen through a maze of dry-docked tuna and charter boats to a small outbuilding where the puppies lived. A salty old gal wearing rubber overalls greeted us.

"You here to see the puppies?" she asked, casually lighting a cigarette.

"Yes, we are," I said.

"They're right over here."

Sporting a noticeable limp in her left leg, she motioned to us to follow her around the corner of the old fishing shack that was surrounded by aged lobster pots and orange buoys to where the puppies were kept in a small, makeshift, wire-fenced yard. They were all sleeping in a great big heap.

"C'mon, you lazy rascals. Time to wake up. You've got company!" the woman barked.

One by one they uncurled themselves from the pile. Some stumbled over to get a drink from the half-empty water bowl; others waddled sleepily over to the fence to see what all the fuss was about.

"Three males. Three females," she continued.

A cute little puppy with tan eyebrows trotted right up to me and wagged her tail. Sometimes it can be just as easy as that. I knew she was the one.

"They're all available except that one," she said, pointing to my first choice. "She's heading out to sea on Thursday. Gonna be a tuna dog." She laughed.

"A tuna dog?" I asked.

"Yep, a tuna captain picked her out yesterday," she said. "How are your sea legs, little rascal?" she joked while tussling the pup's floppy ears. The black and brown puppy that was supposed to be mine backed away.

Needless to say, I was disappointed but went about the task of picking out another.

"How about that one?" Linda said, pointing toward the corner where an ink-black puppy sat all alone. She was smaller than the rest, probably the runt of the litter.

I walked over and scooped her up. She was very cute and shaking with fear.

"It's all right, little girl," I said, trying to comfort her. I've never been able to walk away from the needy ones.

"You want her?" the old sea gal asked gruffly. Obviously, she had some fish to filet.

"Yes, we'll take her," I said.

"Well, good luck," she said and disappeared around the corner.

We brought her back to the cottage, where she quickly ran underneath the bed. I tried to coax her out, but she wouldn't budge.

"I hope this works out," I said.

"Maybe all she needs is some time to adjust," Linda replied.

Now I've been around some insecure puppies and dogs in my life, but this little girl wanted nothing to do with us. Despite my attempts to soothe and assure her, she whined and cried the entire night, not every now and then, but a steady, unyielding series of high-pitched wails and howls of discontent. For whatever reason, the little puppy we had named "Allison" (after Allison Portchnick from Woody Allen's movie *Annie Hall*), was not taking well to her new owners or surroundings.

"We'll have to bring her back in the morning," I said. "Maybe she needs to find a home with one of her littermates." We barely got an hour's sleep that night. There are few things that will frazzle one's nerves more than a puppy whining and crying underneath a bed all night long.

"And there's no way I'm letting that guy take that other puppy out to sea," I said firmly the next morning as we drove back to the docks.

We pulled into the marina again and immediately saw Rosie the Riveter moving some crates around with a forklift. As soon as she saw us approach with Alison, she shut off her machine and jumped off.

"Back again?" she said skeptically, lighting another cigarette.

I explained what had happened the night before and how she might need to be adopted out with another dog.

"Maybe you're right," she grumbled. "She's damn near scared of her own shadow."

"Listen, about that other puppy that the tuna captain wants . . . " I continued.

"Take her," she interrupted. "He backed out yesterday five minutes after you left."

Sometimes "it was meant to be" takes a little work, I thought as we pulled out of the marina and Linda held our new and very happy puppy in her lap. We decided to name her Squeeze.

Unlike Quiche Lorraine, our first cat that made the adjustment from feral life on Long Island to Manhattan apartment cat just fine, Squeeze's conversion to city life was a bit rocky. Granted, trying to house-train a puppy from a ninth-floor apartment, three blocks away from the nearest park and patch of grass, is not the ideal situation, particularly when your new addition is used to the kind of undisciplined freedoms that come with being born in a boatyard. Add to that the challenge of a bladder infection that she'd inherited from Montauk, and we had to abandon any training regimens altogether. For the better part of a month, I had to line our floors with newspapers, as Squeeze had little control over her small bladder because of the infection.

"It's Allison's revenge for our choosing Squeeze over her," I'd joke while spreading that morning's *New York Times* across the wood parquet floors.

We soon learned that what we might have avoided with Allison—the whining, the crying, the fearfulness—would be replaced by a whole new set of personality challenges in Squeeze; namely, stubbornness, defiance, and a serious case of separation anxiety. And in many ways she would turn out to be just as insecure and fearful as Allison had been.

I was familiar with separation anxiety in dogs and had read about its possible causes and solutions. However, I was totally unprepared for Squeeze's first episode when, upon returning from a twenty-minute trip to Zabar's for a cup of coffee, Linda and I found our brand-new, nine-hundred-dollar living-room couch completely ripped to shreds.

A few weeks after the couch massacre, a period of time that included Squeeze's knocking all of our philodendron and ficus trees and their soil onto the dining-room floor when we dared go out to see a movie, I returned to Montauk to pick up some odds and ends at the summer cottage. On my way back, I stopped at the local supermarket, where I saw a young woman taking down the original puppy sign we'd answered for Squeeze.

"Did they all find homes?" I asked while grabbing a shopping cart.

The young woman turned around and smiled.

"As a matter of fact, they did," she said. "Somebody even adopted two of them."

Allison! I thought to myself. A warm feeling of relief washed over me.

"My wife and I adopted one of the females," I said. "We named her Squeeze."

"After the band?" she asked.

"Yep," I replied. "Kind of a silly name, I guess."

"Well, at least they're a really *good* band," she laughed. "How's it working out?"

"Oh, she's great," I said, lying a bit. "She's got some separation-anxiety issues, I think."

"I'm not surprised," the young woman replied, while stuffing the faded sign in her jacket pocket.

"Why do you say that?" I asked, very curious as to her reasoning.

"Her mother was killed two days after she was born," she said. "We had to hand-and-bottle feed all of them from then on." I suddenly felt terrible about scolding Squeeze so severely about repotting our philodendrons.

"That makes a lot of sense," I said quietly.

"Well, it was nice talking with you," she said, heading toward the parking lot.

"Same here."

"Oh, by the way," she called, while removing a flyer from her windshield. "Did my mother show you the puppies?"

"She sure did," I said.

"How was she?"

"Crusty and cranky," I replied.

"That would be my mother," she laughed.

I don't think Squeeze ever liked living in New York City. I'm pretty sure that from day one, she longed to be chasing ducks in the snow instead of dodging buses on Broadway. When we moved to the northern New Jersey suburbs, I saw a marked change in her behavior. And while I can't pinpoint what triggered her transformation from neurotic city dog to semirelaxed suburban dog, it might have been as simple as having easy access to a good-sized yard. Not a big surprise considering her husky/black Lab breed combination, a mix that's more conducive to pulling sleds and fetching wild game than riding the subway. And with the positive change, it sure was nice to be able to go to the local supermarket without fear of her having a coffee table for lunch.

But as Squeeze was my first dog as an adult, I had very high expectations of her. I wanted her to be many things she was not. I would often apologize for her fearful or cautious behavior in the presence of company or guests. I wanted her to be brave. I wanted her to be confident. I wanted her to be relaxed and sure. I wanted her to be the dog in the back of the pickup truck that waits calmly and securely for her owner outside the supermarket.

I wanted her to be the perfect dog.

Yet despite her fears and insecurities, she was always courageous enough to give up what was familiar to tackle another adventure or move. She withstood the most difficult times in the first few years of our marriage, when screaming arguments and slamming doors were almost an everyday occurrence. She also graciously and patiently accepted our baby daughter, Hayden, into the family after almost five years of being our single pride and joy. And she welcomed new dogs and cats into our home with nary a protest or complaint. I will be forever grateful to her for all the sacrifices she made for our young and restless family.

But there is one thing I don't miss at all—her love of trash. Squeeze was obsessed with garbage. I guess it would make sense that a dog born on the docks in Montauk might have scrounging tendencies. We learned early

Squeeze

on, not surprisingly, that she had an affinity for seafood and that empty tuna cans discarded at the bottom of kitchen trash barrels were her favorite fare and she'd go to any lengths to find them and lick them clean.

Scolding her had little effect, and we quickly had to accept that she was a trash dog of the highest (or lowest) order. Nothing gave her more pleasure than rummaging through anything that even vaguely resembled a garbage bag or trash barrel. When we lived in the city, God knows how many times I'd come home from work and find garbage strewn all over the kitchen floor. And Squeeze would be hiding under the bed, guilty as charged.

Her gypsylike scavenging habits only became more pronounced when we moved to the suburbs. On Thursdays, completely aware of the fact that it was trash pickup day in our neighborhood, she'd disappear for hours, her mission triggered by the early-morning sounds of garbage trucks rolling down the street in fits and starts, workers following and oftentimes jogging close behind, lifting and tossing the week's payload into the hungry steel mouth behind. Squeeze, relying on the carelessness of these hurried men or a tear in the bottom of a bag or two, would wait in the bushes until they had moved on and then inspect the area for a rogue steak bone or empty tuna can. It mattered little how well we fed her; she was our very own hobo dog, and this was her hobby, no different from the guy you see on the beach with headphones and a metal detector looking for loose change. The one time I took her to the dump you would have thought we'd arrived at Disneyland.

Squeeze and I journeyed together for ten years. In elevators and city streets. Through snow-laden fields and beneath fiery autumn canopies of sugar maple and oak. Through the birth of a child and the loss of loved ones, she was by my side every step of the way.

In her eleventh year, I asked her to make one more move. It was a difficult one—New York to California. Two dogs, two cats, one five-year-old child, and two adults in search of a new life. It has taken me a long time to forgive myself for maybe asking one move too many.

We'd been in California for a little more than a month. I woke up early as usual and put one-and-a-half scoops of her favorite dry food into a well-worn dish and then dampened the food with warm water so it would be easier for her to eat. The newly shampooed carpets beneath my feet were finally dry. I felt bad that Squeeze had to sleep in the garage that night, but morning came quickly, and I was sure she didn't mind too much. I opened the garage door.

Sometimes, before I fall asleep at night, I can still see her lying there. Too still. Too quiet. I have to focus on something else. Reach for Linda's hand. Look for a sliver of moonlight coming through the window.

My friends were very kind. They assured me that she died peacefully in her sleep.

But Squeeze wasn't supposed to leave so soon. We had too many trails to walk, too many canyons to wander into, too many paths to still go down. And when it was time for her to go, I would be there.

Dear God, I would be there.

woof

CHAPTER **6**

Margarita

ON MY FIRST DAY AS A TEACHER at the Helen Woodward Animal Center, I was given a warning: try to stay away from the lobby on Tuesdays and Thursdays. Since I've always been the kid who had to find out that the stove was hot by actually touching the burner, I went to the lobby on Tuesday that first week. I can appreciate now that the staff was only trying to protect me.

Tuesdays and Thursdays were surrender days at the center, when dogs were returned or given up for adoption. They were the days of bowed heads, forms to fill out, and tearful explanations. They were the days of being left behind—the days of walking away. Often in tears, owners came with many reasons: *I don't have enough time. He has too much energy. We're moving out of state. She's digging up the yard. . . .*

Those first few visits to the lobby burrowed deep into my soul and tested my boundaries of patience, understanding, and compassion. For the first few weeks, I condemned most every man and woman who walked through those lobby doors. But then I remembered how close I had come to walking through those doors one day myself.

When I first adopted my golden retriever, Canyon, and he turned out not to be the "perfect dog," I debated for weeks about walking away.

Tuesdays and Thursdays between 10:00 a.m. and 2:00 p.m. closed that discussion. Once you see the fear, bewilderment, and confusion in the eyes of those animals left behind, you're changed forever.

So when it came time to design a curriculum for my middle school students attending the summer school humane education program, I wanted to include an activity that would leave a lasting impression and insure that only under the most extreme circumstances would walking away be an option.

Breaking the spell that video games, cell phones, and other forms of artificial entertainment have on kids is a mighty task—and my students were no different. Fortunately, dogs and cats offer a potent pathway into young hearts and minds. I wasn't about to pass up an opportunity to teach them a lifelong lesson about being left behind. So on the first day of class, I gave them each a blindfold, a notebook, and a pencil and asked them to follow me out to the dog kennels.

"Why do we need the blindfolds, Mr. Shiebler?" they asked in unison.

"You'll find out soon enough," I said.

I had scheduled the kennel visit during exercise-and-run time for the dogs, and most of the kennels were empty. The kennels were freshly cleaned and washed down, and I led my students down the barren rows of concrete and metal bars, instructing each to choose a kennel that was empty and to stand outside the door. Some students tried to pair up in front of the steel-barred entrances, but I told them otherwise.

"There will be no sharing of the kennels," I said firmly.

Once they had chosen their location, I quietly approached each student, opened the kennel door and instructed them to walk inside and sit down in the middle of the concrete floor. I then closed and locked the steel door behind them. I repeated this procedure with all twenty students until they were all locked inside the kennels.

Once they were inside, with six-foot-high concrete walls on both sides, there was no way for the students to interact. Their only contact with the outside world, other than through the kennel door where they had entered, was through the bars, facing the walkway where the general public could walk by.

"OK, if you haven't done so already, I want you to swing around and face the outside bars," I instructed.

I then walked outside and acted as if I were looking to adopt a dog, stopping to inspect and consider some of the students, pretending to read imaginary kennel cards, lingering for a while in front of some of the cages, completely ignoring and passing quickly by others. After I had made two or three passes, I stopped and asked them how they felt.

"Mr. Shiebler, you hardly even looked at me. You just walked on by!" one student complained. "Why didn't you stop?"

"Now you know how most pit bulls feel," I replied.

"I sure didn't like it when you stopped for a minute and then walked away," another student said. "Just as I was getting my hopes up, you left."

"Exactly," I said.

Next, I asked the students to put on their blindfolds. Knowing how pitch black and silent the kennels turned at night, I could think of no better way for the students to step into the dark life of a dog that's been left behind.

"For the next fifteen minutes, there will be no talking," I said. "I just want you to sit, feel, and listen."

I didn't hear a peep.

Later, when we returned to the classroom, I asked the students to write about their experience in the kennels. A young girl named Kate, who actually loved cats more than dogs, wrote a simple poem about her experience:

It's sad and lonely
It makes my heart start pounding
like I'm going to be alone forever . . .

Words like Kate's are what inspired and propelled me into spending as much time with the newer dogs as possible. Some of them came with

Margarita

memories of home: a favorite blanket, a chew toy, a bone. Some trembled in corners. Others sat motionless, deaf to my tender words and blind to my outreached hands. A few would charge the bars and try to climb the walls, spinning and panting as if they were trying to jump out of their own skins and misfortune. Still others were filled with fury. They were the barers of teeth, the irate barkers and growlers. I used to think of them as the bad dogs, but as time went on I began to see them as warriors. I cheered their defiance and hailed their outrage.

Some dogs handled those first few days better than others. None seemed to have a more difficult time adjusting to the bars and concrete than the Labrador retrievers. The idea of being separated from human contact was almost too much for them to bear. Once inside, their cries for freedom could pierce even the most hardened of hearts.

The border collies and Australian shepherds didn't fare much better. An extremely intelligent and demanding breed that often requires hours and hours of exercise and task-oriented activities, they would literally bounce off the walls when confined to the kennels. Sometimes, it would take weeks for them to calm down enough just to sit still for a few minutes.

Many dogs don't eat for the first few days. Margarita hadn't eaten for five. The first time I saw her, I was captured by her Rusty-like eyes—those warm, emotional, and intelligent eyes so indigenous to shepherds and collies. Her head was cocked to one side, and she had this look that said, *Will someone please just explain to me what's going on here?* So I sat with her. She walked over and sniffed me for a good long time, giving me a thorough background check. I like that investigative quality in a dog. When she was finished, she probably knew what I had eaten for breakfast that morning.

I find the first moments of meeting a new dog fascinating. I have a tremendous respect for the cautious steps and small moves that come with those initial introductions, particularly with the shelter dogs, whose trust has been betrayed or deeply compromised. As a result, I give dogs all the time they need to get to know and feel safe with me.

Margarita was a young shepherd/collie/retriever mix, and her deep brown coat was shaggy and full—a wire-brush wonderland of tangles, mats, and curls. I got the feeling that she was the kind of dog that would still look scruffy no matter how many trips she'd made to the local doggy spa. Perhaps it was the rogue splashes of black fur that dominated her coat or the dirty-brown markings around her mouth and nose that made her look so perpetually disheveled. The stress of her new surroundings had also taken its toll on her overall appearance, as she was shedding huge clumps of fur. The sight of her sitting in the corner, so lost and confused, was heartbreaking.

"Can't blame you for not having much of an appetite, Margarita," I said, leaning my back against the concrete wall. "But you've got to eat something."

I folded my arms and crossed my legs to let her know I wasn't going anywhere soon. I pointed to her food dish and warned her about the column of ants that was rapidly approaching from the northwest corner of her kennel. She came over and sniffed me once more and eventually sat down by my feet. She looked at me. She looked at her food dish. She looked back at me. She walked slowly over to her bowl and began to eat. In between bites, she'd shoot me a glance or two, and if I shifted my body in any way, she'd stop eating.

"I'm not going anywhere," I assured her. She licked the bowl clean, took a couple of sips of water, lay down next to me, and let out a five-day sigh.

ONE OCTOBER NIGHT, I WAS watching television in our living room. It was way past my eight-year-old daughter's bedtime, but I knew that she'd gotten caught up in reading a scary Halloween book that a friend had loaned her.

"Daddy?" she suddenly called out.

"Yes, honey?"

"Oh, nothing . . . " she replied. She was just checking to see if I would be there for the scary parts.

I sat with Margarita for a long while that afternoon—just to let her know someone would be there that day, for the scary parts.

woof

CHAPTER 7

Brody

THERE COMES A TIME IN many single-dog households when the subject comes up of adding a second dog to the clan. "She's lonely and needs someone to keep her company," and "They can play and exercise together" are common reasons. When I brought up the subject one afternoon to my wife, Linda, she came up with a reason that was a little more specific.

"How about having another dog around so our dog will stop eating the furniture?" she suggested.

Noting Squeeze's proclivity for consuming loveseats and small tables when left alone, I set about to find a pal for our separation-anxiety poster child. Following up on an article I'd read in a local newspaper about animal shelters in New Jersey that needed support, we headed down the Garden State Parkway one damp and gloomy Saturday morning to visit one of the less glamorous facilities in the state—the Linden Animal Control Adoption Center.

"We'll just take a look," I promised.

For those of you who have never been to Linden, imagine all the bad things you've heard about New Jersey—oil refineries, industrial waste, air pollution, high cancer death rates, and concrete. And while things have gotten better over the last decade or so, it used to be much worse.

"So much for finding a golden retriever here," Linda said as we pulled into the rundown parking lot. She was probably right. As much as I wanted a golden, I knew what we were up against here—a narrow assortment of less-desirable breeds, the last stop for many.

There's an old saying that warns if you hang around a barbershop, sooner or later, you're going to get a haircut. I have the same problem with animal shelters. Like many dog lovers, I want to take them all home with me. I understand why many people choose to stay away, as shelters can be terribly depressing places. But I've always felt that any amount of love and attention is better than none at all and that a tiny head scratch or soft-spoken greeting might be all a dog needs to make him or her that much more adoptable. It may just take a few minutes to change everything. I know this to be true.

As a young boy, I was terrified of the ocean. During summers when my brother and I went to day camp, we'd take many field trips to the ocean, and I'd often walk along the water's edge, pretending to look for shells, while the rest of my friends frolicked in the breakers. Although I was afraid of the surf, I wanted desperately to be out there with everyone. But despite their urgings and calls, I could never take that first step into the water.

One day, while standing on the shoreline, I felt a hand rest on my shoulder. It was Mr. Campbell, the bigger-than-life director of our day camp. He was a tall, burly man, boisterous and passionate about most everything, and he reached down and took my hand.

"C'mon, pal, let's go," he said, sporting a big smile on his friendly face.

Before I could open my mouth, I was chest high in saltwater.

He must have seen the growing panic in my eyes, and he quickly lifted me up into his arms. I looked out onto the horizon and saw a huge wave heading straight for us. I was convinced that we were both going to die.

"Here's what we're going to do," he said calmly, as I wrapped my arms around his neck in a samurai death grip. "When I count to three, we're going to hold our breath and duck under this wave together." I must have looked at him like he was insane, because he gathered me in a little closer.

"And I promise," he continued, "that if we go under together, we'll come out the other side together."

Before I could say another word, the wave was upon us. We went under together. We came out the other side together. Just as he'd promised. Total time of the experience: Five minutes. One year later, I was surfing in those same waves, a passion that I still embrace to this day.

My point is, the next time you visit a shelter, spend five minutes with a dog. It may make all the difference in the world.

The first time I saw Brody she was curled up as tight as a pincushion in the corner of her concrete-floored kennel. Possibly the saddest-looking creature I'd ever seen, she was the definition of timidity, and it took her a good five minutes to finally make it over to the steel-barred gate where I was kneeling. Once she was close by, I immediately understood my attraction to her. She reminded me of Rusty—the unmistakable eyes of a shepherd, softened by the classic collie colors of orange and white, with feathered wisps of soft fur framing her kind face.

The card hanging above her kennel door estimated her age to be two years. She'd been found in the heavily forested area of south-central New Jersey known as the Pine Barrens, where local residents had seen her wandering around for weeks. Her extreme shyness didn't seem fear based; it had the feel of an animal that had grown up in the wild with little or no human contact. Still, there was an inherent sweetness about her, and less than an hour later, Brody was sitting between Linda and me on the bench seat of our Dodge pickup, heading home.

Not long thereafter, we were to learn that her performance at the shelter that morning was nothing short of Oscar quality. And while she would always remain somewhat shy, little did we know then of the stubborn, hell-raising, passionate dog she'd become.

Brody

With the addition of a new daughter and a new dog, we quickly outgrew our small suburban home. Squeeze and Brody proved to be a perfect match; they became best pals and mischief-makers and needed room to run. So when Hayden was about six months old, we sold our home in Bergen County and moved to a seven-acre farm in the Hudson Valley about an hour outside New York City. It was a beautiful piece of land, with views to High Point State Park in New Jersey to the west and the lovely apple orchards of Warwick to the south.

Here we discovered how much Brody loved the wild things. Nothing thrilled her more than to chase the white-tailed deer that foraged in the meadow below. Although she was fast, she was no match for those hypervigilant leapers and bounders. We would watch her noble but futile chases from our deck, chuckling as the deer would zigzag through the sumac and underbrush and disappear into the woods, leaving Brody behind chasing ghosts.

She would run for hours, seemingly possessed by their phantom scent and trails. When she finally returned home, exhausted, there was a wild glaze in her eyes, and her tongue would be dangling halfway down her chest. Each time, we'd figure that she had finally learned her lesson and would retire from such frivolous pursuits.

No such luck.

On the second night in our new home, Brody decided to bring us a housewarming gift from the meadow. As I was taking out the trash, I heard her unmistakable "I'm on the trail of something" yip and the crackling of twigs and branches in the underbrush. I yelled and called her, knowing damn well she wouldn't come. But after a few persistent growls of my own, she emerged from the brush with something grayish white in her mouth. Although it could have been a disposable diaper for all I knew, I ran toward her, arms flailing in protest to let go of whatever it was. She dropped the object and slunk away. I shined my superstrength, suburban-guy-moves-to-the-country overkill flashlight on the object and was treated to an astoundingly ugly creature full of slobbery fur, fiendish eyes, and a mouth that seemed glued open, baring some pretty impressive spiky teeth.

I quickly went through my New York City and Jersey suburban-wildlife mental database—rat, pigeon, squirrel—and came up empty. And then, suddenly, in the deep dark sky above appeared the kind face of my seventh-grade science teacher, Mrs. Anderson. She gave me a quick refresher course.

"Why, Gary, this is one of our little marsupial friends, the opossum. While he may be virtually undistinguishable right now, that is only because he has spent the last few minutes in the jaws of your dog."

The wise Mrs. Anderson. She was always one of my favorite teachers.

I stood there for a few moments celebrating my first close encounter with a "wild species." Suddenly I saw its jaws move. Not much, but enough to confirm that it was still alive. I scolded Brody hard for not finishing the job and decided the only humane thing to do was to put the opossum out of its misery.

I grumbled as I walked back to the garage, wondering how I might complete the deed. I spotted a baseball bat in the corner and decided it was the best way. The end would be swift, like a walk-off home run with the bases loaded in the bottom of the ninth.

I told myself it was a baptism of sorts, an initiation to the harsh realities of living among the wild things. I grabbed the bat and headed outside. I set my light down on the ground so it outlined the opossum's form. I took a deep breath and noticed that Brody was watching me in a rather curious but bemused way. Mumbling that it was all her fault, I raised my bat above my head. And just as I was ready to lower my thirty-four-ounce gauntlet, Mrs. Anderson's sweet face reappeared in the sky above.

"Now, Gary, this little omnivorous and nocturnal mammal has a very clever way of protecting itself when threatened or attacked. Do you remember what they pretend to do?"

Play dead, I immediately remembered. *Much obliged, Mrs. Anderson.*

I walked back to the garage, grateful that I hadn't clubbed a living animal to death, now understanding why Brody had looked at me the whole time with a puzzled look on her face. I returned about a half hour later to check on the opossum. Sure enough, it was gone.

A few weeks later, Brody and I were on a deep hike on state-forest land. It was a paradise of scents and aromas, and she romped through the waving ferns in search of furry creatures. She ran up ahead in her usual manner, her bark indicating that she was at least lukewarm on the trail of something. All of a sudden, it became more persistent and sharp. I followed the sound into a dark grove of hemlocks and spotted her white-tipped tail wagging furiously. She had obviously cornered something. It was only after she turned around and looked at me that I learned what she had found.

"Oh, Brody, no . . ." I said in disbelief.

What she had cornered was a porcupine who, in turn, had generously deposited thirty or forty needle-sharp quills into Brody's nose, gums, jaw, and tongue. I screamed at her to back away, and she did. The number of quills in her face stunned me. I had heard stories about how most porcupine quills were barbed and almost impossible to remove without a pair of regular or needle-nose pliers. Being two miles deep into state land, I had neither.

Dogs know when they have messed up. You can see it in their eyes. One by one, I pulled the quills out by hand—from her gums, her tongue, the roof of her mouth, her nose, and her chin. She never resisted. She never cried, not even a whimper. After I finished pulling out the last quill, we sat together under the hemlocks for a while. She looked at me with the same sad eyes I first saw at the shelter.

"C'mon, girl," I said. "Let's go home."

That night, when we pulled into the driveway, Brody didn't bolt down into the meadow when I opened the door. She slowly stepped out of the car and dutifully waited for me by the front door. I was convinced she had finally learned her lesson.

No such luck.

One week later, she got skunked. A few weeks after that, she held a raccoon hostage for a couple of hours at the top of a spindly cherry tree. Soon thereafter she got skunked again. I began to wonder if there was any kind of encounter that would make her change her ways.

That following fall, we decided to limit our walks to the open fields and woods behind our home. There, Brody could chase chattering chipmunks, field mice, and gray squirrels instead of porcupines—and I could rest my nerves and enjoy walking in the woods once again. The forest has always been my church, my sanctuary, a reliable refuge. It is where I feel safe, protected, and truly at home.

So when a hunter shot Brody one snowy November morning in the woods behind our farm, I was a homeless man in a world gone mad.

It was a deliberate act. She had been shot at point-blank range on private land where the hunter wasn't supposed to be, illegally trying to bag a white-tailed deer on the last few remaining days of the hunting season. I had heard her barking a ways up ahead, nothing unusual for our hikes, and was calling her to come back when the gunshot exploded. It was followed by a series of heart-piercing yelps and cries.

"Brody!" I screamed in shock. Not a sound. The woods had turned stone silent.

I started running down the trail, desperately calling out her name, frantically searching the dark hollows cloaked by hemlocks and thick groves of pine trees scattered across the hilly terrain. Finally, I found her. She was sitting quietly under a small oak tree, her right paw barely attached to her shattered front leg. I ran over and cradled her in my arms, took off one of my winter gloves, unlaced my boot, and secured the glove around what was left of her paw. I carried her for half a mile out of the woods back home.

She was so much heavier than I remembered. I kept tripping on rocks and branches hidden in the snow and falling down. The gunshot rang over and over in my ears. And she never even whimpered.

The vet said that if the shotgun blast hadn't cauterized all the blood vessels, she would have bled to death.

For weeks, I found myself sitting at traffic lights plotting my revenge. Suddenly, everyone in town that drove a pickup truck with a gun rack became a suspect. Many nights, I drove around the countryside searching for answers I would never find.

The following spring, I went back and stood at the edge of those woods. I had no desire to go back in, but all the pain and anger from that November day poured out of my soul and the sound of my screams ricocheted off every shagbark hickory and hemlock on that hillside. To this day, I have never returned.

It's five years later, and I'm three thousand miles away. A three-and-a-half-legged dog walks by my side on a gently sloping trail just outside our mountain home in Julian, California. We're on a brand-new set of wooded paths and trails, surrounded by species of native pine and oak refreshingly foreign to my eyes. I'm looking forward to getting to know the burgundy-barked bushes called manzanita and the spiky plant local folks call the Lord's Candle.

Suddenly, something flushes out of the brush. A Western ground squirrel, perhaps, but I not quite sure. Brody tenses up for a brief moment and then looks at me with an old gleam in her eyes. But I'm not concerned. She is finished chasing things she can't catch.

And so am I.

woof

CHAPTER **8**

Champ and Yellow Dog

A FRIEND RECENTLY TOLD ME that he had adopted a dog from a shelter.

"What kind?" I asked.

"Oh, I don't know," he replied. "One of those brown ones."

For every purebred Labrador and springer spaniel with papers that came through the center, there were hundreds of "brown ones." They are often the forgotten dogs, the overlooked ones. If people only knew of the treasures hidden behind their common coats and unremarkable features, perhaps they would not pass by so quickly. Whereas the frisky Dalmatian or the adorable teacup poodle may get adopted in a matter of hours or days, the brown ones may have to wait weeks or months for someone to even stop in front of their kennels.

I would like to say that my love of dogs is unflinchingly democratic, that I have no favorites and that I love them all equally. To some degree, this is true. To misquote Will Rogers, I have never met a dog I didn't like. But I'd be lying if I didn't say I'm a bit partial to one particular kind of dog—your basic, all-purpose, garden-variety mutt. And at the Helen Woodward Animal Center, there were many, including two gems—Champ and Yellow Dog.

These two quickly became my number-one choices for my weekly field trips to elementary schools and the many outreach and animal-therapy programs that the center so generously provided for the community. And while it might have been easier to bring a couple of the better-trained or more well-behaved dogs with me, I always felt that Champ and Yellow Dog were the best ambassadors and examples of what gifts and challenges a shelter dog can bring to a home or family.

Champ had spent most of his two-year-long life at the shelter, having been adopted out twice and returned each time.

"Required too much attention," was the explanation of both owners. With excuses like that, I'm sure glad people can't return children.

A shepherd/Doberman mix with a typical blandish coat of tans, browns, and blacks, on the surface, like many of the "brown" ones, he was not the kind of dog that would immediately grab your attention if you casually walked by his kennel. But if you were to stop for a moment or two, like I did one afternoon, you'd quickly discover that Champ was truly a diamond in the rough.

Gazellelike in stature, long-legged and lithe, he moved with the strength and grace of a greyhound with a gorgeous, easy lope, his body athletic and handsome. His almond eyes were always eager and alive, and his ears hung inquisitively from his good, strong head. Most important, through all his hopes and disappointments, there wasn't an angry or bitter bone in his body. He seemed to carry in him an inextinguishable flame of hope. He adored children, and they loved him. He dived and leaped into everything around him, including people's arms and laps, perpetually thrilled by life and all it had to offer. He was like the boy who stands at the very edge of a Grand Canyon overlook, always trying to get a bigger and better look at everything—while his parents scream in horror behind the safety railing.

Forever playful and curious, Champ could usually be found standing on the thin ledge of his kennel where the upper glass enclosure met the lower concrete wall. Like a mountain goat, he'd balance up there for hours, peering over the glass to catch any glimpse of the world outside his kennel. One morning, I arrived at the shelter to discover that Champ had broken the glass above the ledge and it had taken a deep slice out of his leg. When I went to see him in the adjoining animal hospital, his left front paw was bandaged heavily, and his eyes told me that it hurt. One of the vet techs told me that he cut it trying to escape, but I knew he was only trying to get a better view.

On our visits to the schools, he'd bound into the classroom, making the grandest of entrances, his big happy face captivating the young students. It wasn't long before he was completely surrounded by his adoring, newfound friends. Hardly fearful of the overwhelming surge of hands eager to pet and scratch his long and rugged body, he'd simply delight in all the attention, often setting off a flurry of giggles and laughter amongst the children if he chose to bathe an unsuspecting student in sloppy licks and kisses.

Knowing of the nourishment and hope these trips gave him, the hardest thing was bringing him back to his cold, solitary kennel at the end of the day. Sometimes, on our way back to the shelter, I just wanted to keep on driving. It was almost unbearable locking him up behind that steel gate after a day filled with so much attention and companionship.

"I'll be back in the morning, pal," I'd promise each night.

Like Champ, when I was a boy, I hated being alone. I always went to sleep with the radio on. There was something soothing about hearing the voice of a disc jockey, hundreds of miles away in Cleveland or Pittsburgh, coming from the tiny speaker of my portable radio only inches from my ear. With Rusty at the end of my bed, my father only a strong call away (to close the closet door to keep the ghosts out), and the crackling static of an AM radio by my side, the world didn't seem so big, the night so black. My dad, my dog, and my AM radio—the best pals any boy could ask for.

Champ

My dad always used to call me pal. It's an endearing term, one that always made me feel good inside. One of my best pals at the shelter was Yellow Dog.

With a name that could have easily been coined by my father (the same person who lobbied for the name "New Black Kitty" when a gorgeous black Persian wandered into our yard one November morning when I was twelve), Yellow Dog was a wise and weathered old salt who looked like he had spent a few too many nights in port drinking cheap whiskey and chasing the ladies. He'd been found roaming the docks on the eastern end of Long Island, abandoned by a sailor who decided he just couldn't take him out to sea anymore.

"Could have been worse," I said to him on the first day we met. "I once knew a dog that was destined to spend its life on a tuna boat until I came along," referring to another one of my dog pals, Squeeze.

A meat-and-potatoes kind of Lab/hound mix, he was a little rough around the edges and more than a little heavy around the middle. He had a weepy right eye and was starting to gray up a bit around his big, happy mouth. His file said he was four. He and I both knew he was pushing fifty.

A couple of weeks after arriving at the shelter, Yellow Dog developed bloat, a very serious condition in which a dog's small intestine gets twisted. He survived a four- hour operation and spent a good part of his recovery drinking water, eating a little here and there, and resting on the soft carpeting in my office. During that time, I fell in love with the grand, old survivor.

And, oh, how he loved to drink water! Gallons and gallons of water. And he wasn't bashful about letting everyone know how much he enjoyed it. He was the King of Slobber, the Sultan of Slurp. Nothing made him happier than a fresh bowl of cool, clean water.

As nature has it, if you consume a lot of water, you have to get rid of a lot of water. And from Yellow Dog's loins spilled the mighty Colorado. He would douse entire corners of buildings, inundate unsuspecting hedges and tree trunks and flood small parking lots. He had a habit of wagging his tail when he relieved himself, and many times I found myself doing an impromptu jig to avoid getting soaked. Never was taking a dog outside to do business such an adventure.

On one such walk, we ran into a rather stuffy Beverly Hills–type woman. She was pleasant enough but rather haughty, and when she asked me if Yellow Dog was "one of those dogs from the shelter," he looked up at me, casually lifted his leg, and promptly peed on her Donna Karan silk slacks. Naturally, she was horrified. I apologized for his unruly behavior and scolded him the best I could. She stormed away, and we ran to the playfield together, laughing all the way. I'll never know if I waited too long to take him outside or if he was just commenting on the woman's bad attitude. But I have my hunches.

Yellow Dog was one of the few dogs I have known that didn't have some kind of meltdown at the prospect of going for a ride in the car. I

Yellow Dog

have had dogs spontaneously jump into my lap for no reason while I was switching lanes at sixty miles an hour. I've had dogs shed the equivalent of a full winter's coat on a trip to the supermarket. I have spent hours washing nose prints off windowsills and drool off center consoles and dashboards. The sight of a another dog walking down the sidewalk on a leash has sent many of my dogs into a spinning, whining, barking frenzy, usually while I'm trying to negotiate a busy intersection.

Yellow Dog approached car trips in his usual easy manner. There were no big deals in life, and his lazy lope spoke of having seen it all. He made this point of view clear when I took him to a Jewish temple where I was to give a talk to some school children about pet responsibility and care. Knowing that cleaning up after one's pet is a big part of responsible ownership, he decided to enhance my presentation by depositing five very neat piles of business by the *bimah*, the equivalent of Yellow Dog relieving himself on a Catholic altar. The timing and placement couldn't have been worse. Or a point better made about the things dogs do.

Later, I called a good friend, who happened to be a member of the congregation, and told him what had happened. He told me not to worry; he knew the rabbi was a witty and humorous man. Phew.

"He'll probably make Yellow Dog part of the Torah reading of the day," he joked.

The next day, I told Yellow Dog about my conversation. He looked at me with his big, happy face, and we went for a walk.

Just like best pals do.

woof

CHAPTER 9

Cielo

ABOUT A YEAR AFTER WE MOVED to California, I decided to answer a rather ambiguous ad in a San Diego newspaper for a teaching position in Tijuana, Mexico. It was for an after-school program at the Queen Elizabeth Institute, a private school that taught English as a second language to students from surrounding public schools.

I would *like* to say that I got hired because of my sterling résumé and sparkling interview. But I learned later from one of the other instructors that the primary reason I was hired was that I had curly blond hair and blue eyes.

"It is very important to the headmaster at the Institute that the American teachers look American," he told me. As it turned out, they were also looking for someone to teach arts and crafts. My wife had taught art in a number of summer programs back in the States.

"Don't worry," I told her while she was blow-drying her long, blonde hair the night before her interview. "You're a shoo-in."

For the next three years, we would cross the U.S.-Mexican border twice a day, four days a week. Going into Mexico was rarely a problem. Coming back into the United States was often quite an adventure. With the exception of our latest feline addition, Clementine, I have always been the lead culprit when it comes to bringing new creatures into our home. That was until Linda appeared in the Queen Elizabeth school courtyard one day cradling a very dirty, hungry dog that had wrapped its paws around her legs as she stood waiting for a pair of boots in front of a shoemaker's kiosk.

"I've never been hugged by a dog before," Linda beamed. "She wouldn't let go. And isn't she cute? Look at those sweet eyes! And the beard! Look at that beard!" She did indeed have a beard—a very long and scraggly beard. It was the first thing you noticed about her.

In a total role reversal, I gave Linda that "last thing we need is another dog" look as she held the little street terrier in her arms. After all, we already had two dogs and three cats. But I must confess that my resistance was based more on bias than practicality. Until that point, I'd always been a big-dog kind of guy. My experience with little dogs had been limited to two dachshunds when I was a boy—my mom's dog, Juliet, who got hit by a car in front of our house when I was very young, and Phil Roll's dachshund, Dolores, the only dog, to this day, that I've ever known that's received mouth-to-mouth resuscitation.

Not exactly the strongest foundation for a lifetime of passion for smaller breeds.

I was used to being around retrievers, collies, and shepherds. Dogs you could tackle on the front lawn after a long day at school or hug with all your might without fear of hurting them. I had never imagined a small dog being part of our family. Especially one with a beard.

Once word got out that Linda had a little dog in the courtyard, students quickly surrounded us. The little bearded one charmed them all. Linda shared her story about how she had found her.

"She is a gift from the sky, a gift from the sky!" one girl cried out.

So much for finding her a name. We named her Cielo, which was Spanish for "sky." Now all we had to do was get her back home across the border.

Our plan was to hide our bearded contraband under Linda's heavy winter coat on the floor by her feet. In our two years of crossing the border, our car had never been searched. Most of the time we were asked a couple of questions regarding our purpose for being in Mexico and whether we had anything to declare. I remembered seeing a sign once at the border checkpoint that said it was illegal to bring any *produce* or *livestock* into the States. Since a fox terrier didn't fit into any farm-animal category I knew of, we decided that we weren't breaking any laws by trying to bring her home. We felt confident. I would remain cool, casual, and matter-of-fact. Just like on a typical night coming home from work.

We drove from the school to the border crossing at San Ysidro, passing taco stands and young men hawking everything from newspapers to fresh roses. Cielo was curled in a little ball under Linda's parka. She was quiet and still. It was if she knew this was her only chance and wasn't going to blow it.

We jockeyed our way into the typically chaotic line of cars and trucks. Traffic was light, and in minutes we were at the checkpoint. I recognized our border agent; he asked us the usual questions.

"Teaching, sir. Yes, teaching English at the Queen Elizabeth Institute in Las Palmas. Yes, both my wife and myself. No, sir, nothing to declare this evening."

It was a flawless performance. I was brilliantly normal. I had captured and portrayed that kind of day-after-day weariness that comes from crossing the border every day. And Cielo had fallen into nothing short of a coma. Not a squirm. Not a whimper. She knew the stakes.

Now, my wife is the kind of person who always gives away the punch line of a joke at the very beginning of its telling. And then she wants always wants to start over again. So when the border guard asked Linda what was under her coat, my heart went into an instant arrhythmia.

In a tone of voice that would be best described as that of the village idiot, she looked up at the agent and smiled.

"Oh, nothing . . . just my big feet!"

My wife is a beautiful, graceful woman. So when the guard asked her to pick up her coat and she began acting like Marge Simpson, I knew we were doomed. He asked her to step out of the car, walked around to the passenger side, and lifted up her coat. There he found our bearded stowaway, fast asleep.

He said nothing about it. He asked us to get back in the car and tagged a very intimidating little piece of yellow paper to our windshield. He instructed us to proceed to Secondary Inspections, where agents have been known to completely dismantle cars and vans in minutes.

The yellow piece of paper read: *Hiding dog under coat.* We were scared. Not so much for ourselves but for Cielo. Even though she had found Linda only two hours earlier, she was already a part of our family. We couldn't bear the thought of leaving her behind.

My mind began to wander as we waited for the second round of inspections. One of my dreams when I moved to California was to hear the wild howl of a coyote. I realized that dream about a month after I arrived while camping in the desert one night. After dogs and cats, the coyote is my favorite animal.

In Native legends, it is said that Coyote created the earth and carried fire down from the mountains. He was the mischief maker, the trickster, and he could transform himself into any shape he wished. His ultimate responsibility, set down by the Great Spirit Chief, was "to set things right," however he might interpret that mandate. Many of his best-laid plans and schemes didn't turn out the way he'd expected. At those times he used his cleverness and trickery to repair the situation. I thought of Coyote as we sat in that dimly lit holding area.

We waited about an hour. Finally, another border agent approached and asked us to step out of the car. She said very little and asked me to open the trunk. She poked around a bit with her flashlight and then plucked the yellow piece of paper from the windshield. She looked at it for a moment and with a wave of her hand told us to proceed across the border.

I don't think she heard a word of my story about how I had brought "Freckles" down to Mexico to teach my students a lesson about dog physiology. Just one look at Cielo and she would have known I was lying.

The next day when I shared the story with my fourth-grade class, the same little girl that had given Cielo her name explained to me why the border agent let us go.

"Why is that?" I asked.

"Because she knows what a gift from the sky looks like," she said with a big smile on her face.

Once home, Cielo was accepted into our pet family with scarcely a protest. But there was one notable exception.

In the great tradition of dogs not getting along with cats, Cielo became the torchbearer for such strained relationships, his costar being the John Wayne of our cat enclave, Mitten.

To this day, I still can't figure out what the problem was. Except for his epic street battles with our big male tomcat, Midnight, Mitten was easygoing and nonconfrontational. He got along fine with Squeeze, Brody, and Canyon, and his relationship with our other cats, Rainbow and Lucy, was mostly that of a patient but firm big brother.

But when it came to our peppery firecracker of a Mexican import, there was tension the moment Cielo walked in the front door. Always moments away from a confrontation or scuffle, the relationship between Mitten and Cielo was pure opera—a masterpiece of drama and intrigue that could explode at any moment with a simple glance or well-placed flick of a tail into a Carmenesque barrelhouse brawl. It was our very own dog vs. cat libretto, and we were usually guaranteed one performance a day.

Mitten seemed to have Cielo's number, always knowing what button to push. The end of our bed was eternally contentious turf, and many a morning Linda and I were awakened by a full-on riot of snarls, growls, and swipes—Cielo often reduced to the likes of an abandoned Mexican snapping turtle—as Mitten would calmly walk out of the bedroom. It was as if they had some kind of twenty-four-hour-a-day telepathic feud going on—a silent, irresolvable disagreement privy to themselves and no one else.

Cielo

I will say this: when Mitten got sick, everything changed. As his dementia from feline leukemia worsened, he would wander about endlessly throughout the house, sometimes getting stuck in corners, unable to figure how to get out. It was Cielo that would often help Mitten, sidling up to him and brushing her head against his whiskers to help him with his bearings so he could turn around. It's a shift in behavior that I've seen many times with my pets; compassion awakens when one of their clan is in need. It can be both inspiring and heart-wrenching at the same time.

While many of my dogs and cats have shared in a fair amount of pain and trauma over the years—Brody getting shot in the woods, Canyon contracting cancer at the unbearably young age of seven, Mitten's encounter with the steel fox trap, and Spencer meeting his demise at the hands of a pack of coyotes—Cielo's life with us has been relatively free of drama. I think she must have paid off those dues during her first three years living on the streets of Tijuana. It's hard to see those memories rise up sometimes.

For example, while she's fine with any kind of physical contact with Linda or Hayden, she still flinches when I reach down to pat her head or scratch her back. This leads me to believe that she was kicked or smacked by one of the many—mostly men—street vendors she hung around while in Mexico. And Linda recently pointed out that when I'm preparing dinner for her, Cielo will rarely look up at me, always focusing her attention on the floor beneath my feet, where, as on the street, something might fall or drop in front of her to eat. It is a touching reminder of where she came from and the life that many homeless dogs still lead across the border.

Despite her sweetness and charm, she is one of the toughest cookies I've ever known. I've seen her go after dogs three times her size and once, when a Doberman appeared on our front lawn, barking and threatening Linda, who was outside gardening, I thought Cielo was going to chew right through the thick-screened security door to protect her. The Doberman took off and was never seen again.

While there's no doubt that Cielo loves me, it wouldn't be an understatement to say that our bearded bundle of sweetness absolutely worships Linda and Hayden. There have been times when Linda has come home from work and Hayden from school at the same time when I was convinced that Cielo, so smitten and overwhelmed by their simultaneous arrival, was going to faint on the spot. Like a schoolgirl at a Justin Timberlake concert, Cielo's reaction to them is one of pure adoration. I have never seen a dog love two people more. To this day, she still sleeps at the foot of Hayden's bed, patiently waiting for her to come home, even though she's been gone at college almost a year.

"Why don't you just rip my heart out of my chest?" Linda will often say to Cielo when she walks by Hayden's room, she missing our twenty-one-year-old daughter as much as her curled-up friend does.

For years, Cielo was our personal bedsheet and foot warmer. Who needs an electric blanket when you can let your dog under the bedcovers about half an hour before bedtime? She loved sleeping in her little cave, and her small form was never intrusive. She truly kept us warm on those extra chilly winter nights.

Sadly, at almost fifteen years old, she's not strong enough to jump up or down off the bed anymore. I hate it when my dogs get old.

Over the years Cielo has lost her appetite for canned dog food—probably because I've spoiled her with so many treats. She'll still eat dry food, especially if I wet it down a bit with some chicken or beef broth. She's a bone-and-doggie-jerky fiend and will often sit at my feet until I give in, looking up at me with that irresistible, happy bearded face.

"How many bones have you given her this morning?" Linda will ask.

"One hundred and twenty-six," I'll reply. "I can't help myself."

Once a week I'll cook up some bacon just for her, break up the strips into little bite-size pieces, and then pour the remaining grease over her dry food. She goes nuts.

"You know the moment we brought you across the border, you hit the lottery," I'll tell her as she gobbles down her dinner.

So did we.

woof

CHAPTER **10**

Frazier and Parson Brown

HE GREETED ME WITH A WARY snarl, a cautious glare, and a low growl.

Frazier frightened me. But for some reason, I didn't walk away.

I take an instant liking to certain dogs. Others I approach with the same kind of wariness with which Frazier approached me. Either of those kinds of beginnings can grow into long and rewarding relationships. So I didn't rush to judge his reaction to me. I didn't try to force good nature upon him. I respected his need to give me a thorough going-over. After all, I was a very risky investment. His previous owners had walked away only hours before he and I met.

His skin was flaky dry, his fur lifeless. He was sickly thin—haunches too wiry, undernourished, and obviously underloved. Originally a street dog, "Perro de Calle," as they say in Tijuana, he was a chow/husky mix, a wary and somewhat mysterious breed combination to say the least. Chows were originally bred in China as palace guard dogs. Huskies like to pull sleds in subzero temperatures over great distances. It's not surprising that he didn't work out in that Pacific Beach condo.

It took a long time before he softened. Our courtship was awkward—an endless first date with lots of well-intentioned fumbling and missteps. When he finally started letting me into his kennel, he would leap up to greet me before I even got his gate closed. I would yell "OFF!" push him away, turn around to pick up his food dish, invariably trip on a blanket or chew toy, and fall down on the concrete floor. Frazier, taking full advantage of my tumble, would then jump into my lap and I'd find myself hugging him—half out of desperation, half out of sheer love and affection.

Once in my lap, he'd playfully gnaw on my hands and wrists with his surprisingly soft mouth. I would yell "NO!" and he'd comically collapse on his back, his belly fully exposed to the sky and his feet splayed in four cockeyed directions. We would both laugh—I with lungs and throat, he with eyes and tail. Our relationship was not too dissimilar to a few of my first high school romances—clumsy and tender.

A couple of months after Frazier arrived, he was diagnosed with kennel cough, a common but very infectious condition that can easily spread to other dogs. He was quarantined. I didn't see him for the better part of three weeks.

When he emerged a few weeks later, something had changed. Can a prisoner thrown into solitary emerge healthier and stronger? Can "time in the hole" ignite some kind of deep renewal? What I saw was a different dog. His skin, beneath shiny fur, was pink and vibrant, and there was a new sparkle to his eyes. His body had filled out beautifully during his isolation, and he looked strong and healthy. Perhaps the combination of good food and rest was just what this former Tijuana street dog needed.

He was still rowdy and unpredictable, and he still disliked men who wore baseball caps and had beards, but he seemed to recover something in his solitude. Perhaps it was as simple as the restoration of his confidence and dignity, something that he'd lost or never even had on the streets of Tijuana. A street dog knows the street. Nothing else.

Two weeks after he had been released from quarantine, he was adopted. I was both astounded and elated. However, even with all his improvement, both physical and behavioral, I had my doubts about his adoptability, mainly because of his constant struggle to control himself. He just overloaded too quickly, and I worried about his being put into a place or situation he couldn't handle.

Fifteen days later my fears were realized. Frazier was returned. He had become aggressive toward some children at a crowded public beach. Overwhelmed and afraid, he had tried to bite a boy that had inadvertently backed him into a corner. The next morning, the decision was made to put Frazier to sleep.

While it was extremely rare for a dog to be put down at the center, biters always faced that possible fate. Save a possible rescue from someone on staff, there was no way a dog designated as a biter could be adopted out with any degree of confidence that it wouldn't happen again. And even though the number of dogs put to sleep was less than half of 1 percent of the thousands of strays and surrenders that came through the center, it never made those decisions any less agonizing. They were the darkest hours of the darkest days at the shelter. When a dog is returned to the shelter for biting, the other dogs seem to know. An eerie awareness always settles over the kennels during those times.

I sat with Frazier the day he was returned. He was his usual crazy self, excited by everything, barely able to process all the information and stimulation around him. We greeted each other with our signature assortment of cha-chas and playful scuffling, and we ended up tumbling to the floor together as usual. I sat on his tattered blue blanket. He brought me his ball and collapsed in my lap. Stopping play for a moment, he looked up at me with his always willing eyes. I held his head in my hands and then gently stroked his chest. He began to wind down like a tired clock and for a few moments was still and peaceful. I began to cry, and like so many dogs before him, he let me. I told him that it just wasn't going to work out this time but that his heart was too big and good not to carry on in some way. It was all I could think of.

Perhaps it sounds foolish, but I know I will meet Frazier again someday, whether it's in the eyes of a silly puppy stumbling all over itself

Frazier

or in the determined gait of a street dog searching for food. Or in the howl of a newcomer behind a kennel door.

Frazier was put to sleep the next morning at 11:00. The kennels fell silent. It would be easy to say that it was just a coincidence. But I know better than that. The rest of the day was a blur, a mix of emotions ranging from helplessness to anger. The staff warned me that bad days often came in bunches. The next morning, I would see that they were right.

His history read like a criminal rap sheet. *Breed: Jack Russell terrier. Third failed adoption. Had bitten new owners five times. Very dominant and aggressive, particularly around food. Attacked puppy and refused to let go. Growled at kennel techs trying to clean floors. Extremely unpredictable. Owners have "tried everything."*

. . . Except letting him be a Jack Russell terrier.

I knew twenty minutes of Parson Brown's life. Two days before we lost Frazier, Parson Brown had also been returned to the center for the last time. He had refused to eat and hadn't relieved himself since he'd arrived. One of my coworkers said he was waiting to "let it all go at once." Parson Brown had become somewhat of a leper. His reputation was such that no one wanted to go near him. But bad reputations interest me, and I wanted to find out for myself how horrible he really was.

With Frazier still heavy on my heart and mind, I went to see Parson Brown. I slowly opened his kennel door. I carefully hooked his leash. We went for a walk together. We walked across the parking lot on our way to the playfield. A large garbage truck pulled in the driveway. Parson froze, lifted his right front paw, pointed his small stump of a tail, and assessed the situation. No immediate threat. We moved on. His gait was strong, confident, and purposeful. He began to pull a bit on his leash. I gave it a sharp tug. He respectfully slowed down. He wanted to go right; I pulled him left. We played chess with each other—I watched his moves and he watched mine. He had his reputation; I was giving him a taste of mine.

Once we arrived at the field, there was work to be done—scents to be identified, territories to be defined. Things to be protected and enemies to be found. He approached ground-squirrel and gopher holes like a policeman with a warrant. Nose in. No fear. Just checking the situation. He moved from hole to hole with SWAT-team precision. He was patient and thorough. When he felt satisfied with his inspection, we moved on. He pulled right; I pulled left.

White queen takes black rook.

I sat on a bench under a tree that was dying, a barren reminder of the drought that has gripped the area for the last couple of years. Parson sat at my feet. I closed my eyes and pictured a ranch in Wyoming, one that resembled the photograph I had hanging in my office—thunderheads building in the western hills, red-tailed hawks carving circles in the air and screaming in celebration of the endless sky above, cattle grazing, and sunflowers swaying in the breeze.

I opened my eyes. Parson was looking at me. We made eye contact for the first time. I introduced myself. He did the same with a barely noticeable wag of his short and sturdy tail. I patted his side firmly and affectionately as he turned around to resume his guard over the field.

Parson Brown

I closed my eyes again and found myself back in Wyoming. The prairie wind felt gentle and strong at the same time as it combed the tops of the wild grasses. The afternoon shadows grew longer as the sun began its slow autumn descent in the western sky. The distant hills became a tinted peach. It took a long time, but I realized I'd finally found a place to call home. Soon, I'd be chopping wood for the evening fire.

I opened my eyes, and Parson Brown and I began to move again. Walking quietly at first, the small, proud hunter soon gave chase to a jackrabbit that sprang from the brush, but the rabbit was too fast.

"Maybe next time," I say. "Maybe next time."

woof

CHAPTER 11

Canyon

WHEN I WAS A BOY, EVERY morning before school my father made lunch for my brother and me. I can still see him standing in the kitchen in his pajamas, listening for baseball scores on the dusty radio that sat atop our refrigerator while he carefully assembled our sandwiches. Some days it was Virginia ham and Swiss cheese with mustard; other days we got bologna or roast beef with mayonnaise on a soft Kaiser roll. If we were really lucky, we'd unwrap our aluminum foil at school to discover last night's sirloin-steak leftovers between two slices of Wonder Bread with plenty of salt, pepper, and mayonnaise and a dash of Lea & Perrins. Each lunch held a tender reminder of how much our father loved and cared for us, and we were rarely disappointed.

Sometimes, hidden among the tiny red boxes of Sun-Maid raisins and plastic bags filled with vanilla wafers, we'd find little notes or baseball scores. My dad knew that Roberto Clemente was one of my favorite baseball players, so he always made sure to let me know how many hits he had had the night before.

"Three for three," his little yellow note might say.

These days, supermarkets offer a wide assortment of premade lunches and snack packs for children. Packaged in bright and cheery boxes, they are easy, convenient, and require no preparation. They may contain anything from minisandwiches, small squares of cheese, tiny stacks of lunchmeat, bite-size cookies, brownie chunks, to even miniature do-it-yourself pizzas.

After Squeeze died, I vowed that the next dog I got would be independent, sure, and strong. Having lived with a very fearful and insecure dog for eleven years, I was determined to find something that was much more low maintenance in temperament and nature. I wanted a dog on the order of those prefab lunches—bright and cheery, neat, compact and tidy, convenient and easy. I didn't find one. In fact, I ended up with the exact opposite of what I was looking for—a big, goofy, fearful mess of a golden retriever named Canyon.

"If the choice of dogs is a true reflection of their owner, I'd be concerned if I were you," Linda quipped.

I got Canyon about a month after Squeeze died. I felt guilty about looking so quickly. I probably rushed into it too soon. I just got tired of missing her.

Canyon was the first dog I looked at. The ad said: BEAUTIFUL YOUNG MALE GOLDEN RETRIEVER. AKC, $40.00. My daughter, Hayden, and I went to see him.

He had been dumped in a side yard and ignored for the better part of his one-and-a-half years. When his owner walked him to the front yard, it was as if Canyon was seeing the outside world for the first time. A voice inside me said, "Run away! He's too much work! Run away!" But I stayed and ventured in a little deeper.

Such searches are deep affairs of the heart, and there seems to be a point of no turning back. Once I cross the boundary between caring and not caring, it's impossible for me to retreat into indifference. The moment I saw this terrified and neglected young dog, I was doomed. I felt a deep sense of responsibility and duty that I couldn't possibly ignore. It was clear that if I didn't take him, he would be returned to a place of unimaginable loneliness, abandonment, and despair. I couldn't walk away.

Even though I'd already made up my mind, I decided to take him for a trial walk around the block. He startled at almost everything—the rustle of a leaf in a tree, the slam of a car door, even the errant shuffle of my feet on the sidewalk. He almost leaped into my arms at the sight of a black garbage bag sitting at the end of one of the driveways. He was like a newborn colt walking on a trail of rattlesnakes. I wondered whether he had left that side yard at all. I sat down on the curb and slowly pulled him over. My gentle pats and soft scratches echoed my daughter's promise.

"Don't worry, Canyon," she whispered. "We will take care of you."

We took him home. My wife, practical and sensible to the core, was visibly disappointed. To her, he was a "big project."

"We don't need any more big projects," she lamented.

For weeks, I tried to convince her of his good points.

"You know, honey, he really is surprising me with his intelligence."

I kept trying.

"You know, sweetheart, you may laugh, but beneath that dopey demeanor is a very smart dog. And don't forget, he is registered with the AKC."

"American Knucklehead Club," she said, without skipping a beat.

I couldn't argue. He was a complete and total knucklehead.

Up to that point, rarely had I seen a golden that could not at least half-gracefully retrieve a stick or catch a ball. I had to stop playing fetch with him for fear he would seriously injure himself running into a tree or a side of a building. Many times, I'd throw the ball maybe five feet into the air, only to watch him masterfully miscalculate his jump and land flat on his back. He was an expert at running at least twenty-five feet past a freshly thrown stick, and once he tried to turn around on a small walking bridge at a county park and fell off into the dry riverbed below.

We decided to leave him home on our first trip to the Grand Canyon.

While he certainly had coordination issues outside the house, inside he was our very own bull in a china shop.

Canyon

When it came to potted plants, Christmas ornaments, and cups of tea, Canyon's tail was a lethal weapon. He could easily clear off an entire coffee table's worth of books and cocktails with one swipe. Even small children were fair game if they accidentally crossed the path of one of his wagathons.

The sound of a leash would reduce him to a series of convulsive fits and tremors. And trying to put a collar around his neck was nothing short of a vaudeville routine. He'd sit for a second, jump up, sit down again because he knew it was wrong to jump up, then try to jump into his collar like a circus dog through a flaming hoop, miss completely, sit down again, shake, whine, tremble, belch, look at me, look at the door, look at me, look at the door, look at me. . . .

Even the other dogs watched in disbelief.

Once I got his collar on, getting from the kitchen to the front door was an adventure in and of itself. The combination of paws and toenails on the linoleum floor was very similar to the skating clowns segment at the Ice Capades. There was no talking sense or calm into him when he wanted to go outside.

Once, during a well-intentioned training session, I tried to make him sit inside the doorway with hopes that he might gather himself before we headed out. It was too painful to watch. He looked like a chicken that was about to lay a dozen eggs.

I have known and lived with a number of golden retrievers throughout the years, and I am fully aware of their hearty appetites and nondiscriminatory palates. I have seen them devour entire turkey breasts and pumpkin pies set too close to the edges of countertops, swipe sticks of butter from dinner tables, and inhale bowls of cat food in a matter of seconds. Of all the breeds, they are perhaps the biggest scroungers.

A few months after my childhood dog, Rusty, died, my mom and dad got the first of their many golden retrievers. They named her Honey, a name usually associated with sweetness, humility, and love.

I understand that any dog brought into my family after Rusty died would have a tough row to hoe, particularly with me. But to suddenly have a dog that expected the world to revolve around her twenty-four hours a day was quite a shock, especially when compared to Rusty's unselfish and heroic personality. Honey was as haughty and demanding as any dog I've ever known, and if you dared not give her attention, she would stand stubbornly at your feet and remain there until you petted her.

Admittedly, she was golden gorgeous. But, oh, did she know it.

In her defense, my dad didn't help matters much. He doted upon her every wish and desire. He used way too many P-words around her. Precious. Pretty. Princess. Priceless.

"How about 'Pathetic'?" I would chime in, regarding their behavior.

They both, of course, ignored me.

When it came to eating things, Honey was nothing short of a barnyard goat. She would eat *anything*. Aside from my mother's pantyhose, one of her favorite delicacies, she had a fondness for plastic toys and dolls, once devouring an entire pink hula-hoop that my younger sister had received one Christmas morning. Needless to say, my parents ended up at the emergency room of the animal hospital later that night.

"So, what is it this time?" the always good-natured Dr. Barry would ask whenever Honey showed up with a bellyache.

I don't think I'll ever forgive her for eating half my baseball card collection. The thought of her snacking on my Mickey Mantle rookie card is almost too much to bear. Canyon was no better. While showing little interest in my wife's lingerie, he did have a penchant for running shoes, teddy bears, and small area rugs.

Like Squeeze, Brody and so many other dogs I have known, Canyon was most happy when chasing seagulls at the beach or galloping along trails in the forest. It was during those wild and liberating times that his true nature emerged. He would shed his clumsy ways, and many of his fears and uncertainties would magically evaporate into the open skies above. He'd become wise to the world around him—the air, the light, the earth beneath his feet. He was free. Free to do the things that dogs love to do.

Those were our happiest times together.

When I first got Canyon, I was angry and disappointed that he wasn't the dog I wanted him to be. I wanted him to be the perfect dog. But no matter what I said or did, he never changed. I tried to fix him. I stocked up on dog-training books. I sought counsel from friends who had similarly unruly dogs. I bought instructional videos and took him to countless obedience classes. Nothing worked.

Three months after I got him, frustrated and defeated, I considered putting Canyon up for adoption. I was convinced that every dog on the other side of every fence was more obedient, better behaved, and less fearful than my own.

Then I started teaching at the animal shelter, where I met hundreds of dogs like Canyon. Dogs that jumped up too much. Dogs that had too much untamable energy. Dogs that barked too much. Dogs that were too much work. Dogs like Frazier and Champ and Cody. Orphans in a world filled with too many expectations and too little time. How close Canyon had come to being one of them.

And so I sat down with him one afternoon on our front porch, took his sweet face into my hands, looked into his eyes, and made a promise that I would never, ever give up on him. That's all any dog wants to hear. That day, I stopped searching for the perfect dog and started loving the one I had.

From that moment on, everything changed. I'm not going to say that Canyon suddenly turned into Lassie or Rin Tin Tin. He still had no clue as to how to retrieve a ball or stick. He still had nervous breakdowns at walk time. And in spite of the fact that he'd been "fixed," he still loved to mark the end of our mattress and box spring set on a regular basis. But he sure seemed much more comfortable and secure in his own skin. Perhaps the knowledge that I would never walk away was all the incentive he needed to start becoming the dog both he and I wanted him to be.

He will never be the dog who waits patiently in the back of my pickup truck while I sip coffee with a couple of buddies at the local diner. He will never be a finalist in any Frisbee-catching contest. He will most likely not be the dog that sits obediently at my feet while I relax in my favorite chair reading the latest issue of *Western Horseman*. He will never be the fearless, majestic, heroic dog of my dreams—the perfect dog.

But then, I will never be the perfect owner.

What a relief.

I FELT THE LUMP UNDER his shoulder while brushing him one Saturday morning. At first I wasn't concerned, thinking it might be a fatty deposit or the like. But when a similar growth appeared in the same spot on the opposite side of his body, I decided to have it checked out. I was completely unprepared for the news I received a few days later.

"Canyon has lymphoma," the vet told me on our return visit. "I'm sorry."

My options were few. With chemotherapy, he might survive a year, no longer. Untreated, I was looking at four to six weeks.

"But he's only seven," I said weakly.

Linda and I decided to forego the chemotherapy. Depending on the dog, the side effects could be as devastating as the illness itself. I had my hunches about Canyon.

He went downhill so fast. Less than a month later, he was gone.

There is a ridge in the mountains outside of Julian where the moist breezes off the Pacific meet the dry winds rising up from the Anza Borrego desert below. The result is a landscape rich with elements of each. Tall lodgepole pines and lush Engelmann oaks mingle with sagebrush and cactus, and there's always a sweet, briny aroma to the air that is both calming and invigorating at the same time. It is a place Canyon and I hiked many times. Under the sunniest of skies or the grayest canopy of clouds, we'd walk together, him never straying too far ahead, me always enjoying how his golden coat blended in with the sandy soil. I always carried a canteen, and when we'd stop to rest in a shady spot, he'd gladly drink from the small, leaky spring of water that I'd poured inside my cupped hands. It was a good five-mile loop, but we never tired of walking it together. At the very top of that trail is where I would say goodbye.

I held the small cedar box that housed his ashes in my hands. It was a perfect day on the ridge. Not quite knowing what to do, I opened the box and held it high above my head.

"Here ya go, boy," I said. A gentle but firm breeze picked him up, and he flew away in four different directions.

Just like Canyon.

woof

CHAPTER 12

Dirk, Wolfy, and Molly

THE DAY MY DAUGHTER WAS born, a man who had been lost most of his life finally found a purpose. Everything up to that point had been a temporary distraction at best. And while the pregnancy and birth was an extraordinary experience, it was the minutes, hours, days, weeks, months, and years of loving and raising my daughter that molded me into the man I am today. From the moment I held Hayden in my arms, I knew what I was supposed to do.

I delighted in my daughter's company. Whether it was going for a walk in the woods with Squeeze and Brody or taking a nap together in the hammock on a perfect summer's day, I cherished most every moment with my little girl.

One of the things we enjoyed most was reading together, especially before bedtime. On our weekly excursions to the library, it was not uncommon for us to check out the maximum twenty picture books. When we ran out of titles at our local library, we'd just hop in the car and head to another branch.

While we both had our favorite authors and illustrators, Hayden loved any stories that had to do with animals, particularly cats and dogs. Like most kids her age, she loved Clifford and Garfield. But the real treasures were to be found in the older and out-of-print titles, books that featured the most intricate drawings, colorful paintings, and fanciful illustrations, thoughtfully bound and worn from years of use. There was a timeless magic in those wise and weathered pages, and we couldn't wait to get home to get lost in their beautiful pictures and fertile stories.

As Hayden grew older, her love of reading continued, and when she reached the fifth grade, she was assigned a book that would become one of her all-time favorites, *Island of the Blue Dolphins*. Little did we know how important that book would become in *all* our lives.

The year we decided to move to the mountain community of Julian just east of San Diego, Hayden was entering the sixth grade. We thought it would be a nice transition from elementary school, starting junior high school anew. It didn't take us long to find a house to rent close to the center of town—a spacious cedar chalet with big glass windows overlooking the valley. It was the perfect transition house, not too isolated but still very mountain and country in feel. It was even walking distance to Hayden's new school.

With less than two weeks to go before our August 1 move-in date, we decided to take a short vacation back east to visit my family on Long Island. Two days into our trip, I got a call from our realtor in Julian.

"The owner got an offer on your rental house that he couldn't turn down," she said. "He's decided to sell."

Everything in our old house in San Diego was boxed up and ready to be moved the weekend we returned from New York. And while I would have preferred to focus my attention on soft-shell crabs and Manhattan clam chowder, we had to find a new place—fast. Not an easy thing to do when you're three thousand miles away.

I asked my realtor to scour the local newspapers, bulletin boards, and MLS listings. She called me back half an hour later.

"I just got a call from a woman in Pine Hills who's got a house on three acres that's been on the market for a while, and she's thinking about . . ."

"We'll take it," I interrupted.

"Don't you want to see it?" she asked.

"No," I said, thinking about our garage filled with boxes. "We'll take it."

It would be the second time I'd rent a house in California, sight unseen. I was hoping we'd have as much good fortune with this one as we did with the first.

"By the way," I asked, "how far is it from the middle school?"

"About five miles or so," she said.

"Are there any kids in the neighborhood?" I continued.

"Well, it's not like the first place," she said. "The houses are more spread out. However, there is a pretty famous Julian resident right down the road from you."

"Who is that?" I asked.

"Dorsa O'Dell," she said. "Her husband wrote a children's book called *Island of the Blue Dolphins*. Have you ever heard of it?"

I paused for a moment as Linda handed me a plate of Long Island baked clams.

"We'll take it," I said.

Dorsa O'Dell's home, Stone Apple Farms, is the kind of house you pass by on a Sunday drive through the country and declare unequivocally, "That's where I want to live someday." It used to be an old packing house for one of the largest apple orchards in Julian, and its stone foundation, brown-shingled exterior, cedar-shake roof, and circular driveway that's always lined with daffodils in the spring make it the country home everyone dreams of. Hayden and I paid a visit shortly after we moved. A small but sturdy older woman was digging in a flower box by the front screen door.

"Mrs. O'Dell?"

"It's Dorsa," she snapped. "And who wants to know?" she said, barely looking up.

"My name is Gary, and this is my daughter Hayden."

"And?" she said.

"Well," I stammered, "we're your new neighbors, and I just wanted to stop by to introduce ourselves."

"Double vomit!" she said, standing up to take a quick look at us. "The only reason you're here is because you found out that my husband is Scott O'Dell. You wouldn't happen to be a writer, would you?"

Nothing like being busted by a ninety-year-old woman.

Thankfully, just as I was looking for a small hole to crawl into, three huge dogs barged through the screen door and galloped into the front yard.

"Dirk! Wolfy! Molly!" Dorsa yelled. "Get back here!"

The three potential fugitives stopped dead in their tracks.

"What do you write about?" she continued.

"I'm working on a book about dogs," I replied.

"Well," she said, setting down her garden trowel. "Now we have something to talk about."

THERE ARE FEW THINGS MORE endearing than the bond between dogs and their owners. Particularly when it comes to people like Dorsa O'Dell and her "kids." But often, the bonds between dogs can be equally inspiring. It wasn't uncommon to have pairs of dogs surrendered at the shelter. Shadow and Spirit came in as brother and sister. Roofey and Jonesy came in as inseparable pals. In the case of Chaz and Sunshine—as I would discover with Wolfy and Molly—there was little doubt about their relationship; they were husband and wife. Imagine Hume Cronyn and Jessica Tandy—with fur.

Chaz and Sunshine had been adopted from the center six years earlier and returned because their owners were moving out of state. Of all the dogs that had been returned while I was teaching, their return was the hardest to accept. Yet, despite being left behind at such an old age, they demonstrated a remarkable air of acceptance and dignity, their

Chaz and Sunshine

loyalty and love for each other cushioning the shock of their fate and new surroundings. They were an inspiration to us all.

Chaz was a big, barrel-chested Akita mix. Gentle, quiet, and occasionally grumpy, he had one purpose in life: to watch over Sunshine. They had been together for almost seven years, which translates into almost fifty years of human companionship.

He was still crazy about her, and it showed. Every time I entered their kennel, I had to pass his inspection. There was no visiting his Sunshine without his permission. Once I was inside, he'd give my legs, hands, and body a thorough sniffing over. If everything checked out, he would slowly escort me to her blanket. Never leaving my side, he'd stand and wait patiently until my audience with his beloved queen was over. Up to that point in my life, I'd never been chaperoned by a dog before.

Chaz attended to Sunshine's every need. If other dogs got too rough with her on the playfield, he would let them know it with a quick snap or growl. He would also occasionally bark at children passing by their kennel, especially if they were making too much noise as if to say, *Keep it down, you little whippersnappers! Can't you see the little lady is trying to take a nap?* He was just taking care of his woman.

The object of his abiding love was a nine-year-old retriever/bloodhound mix. Reserved and faithful, Sunshine often feigned frailty in light of all Chaz's pampering, but she knew very well how to take care of herself. If I happened to give Chaz a little more attention than I gave her, she would quietly walk over, shoo him away, rest her chin on my lap, and politely demand her fair share of head scratches. Still, it was a joy to watch their dance and to see how much they relied upon each other every day to make it through. Their dependence was not a weakness. They just knew that they didn't have the strength to do it alone.

A generous couple that had been married for over thirty years eventually adopted Chaz and Sunshine. The two old dogs left the Helen Woodward Animal Center one sunny afternoon just as they had arrived—together.

"THAT'S DIRK, THAT'S MOLLY, AND that's Wolfy," Dorsa pointed out as Hayden and I stood on the brick walkway.

"They're quite a crew," I said.

"You're going to have to speak up," she barked. "I can't hear worth a darn."

"I SAID THEY'RE QUITE A CREW!"

"You don't have to yell," Dorsa snapped. "Now, let's take a look at you."

She walked toward Hayden and me and put on her glasses.

"These are my ogre glasses," she said. "Not the most attractive things, but I'm legally blind, and it's the only way I can read."

The left side of her glasses was indeed "ogrelike." There was a round bubble resembling a magnifying glass in the middle of the lens. She leaned in about six inches from Hayden's face and started looking around.

"My, you are a beautiful girl," she said. "Now, let's take a look at your father."

She walked right up to me and asked me to lean over.

"Hmmm . . . curly hair . . . blue eyes . . . a good nose and a bad liar," she said.

"You got me," I laughed.

"Wasn't hard," she said.

I knew I was going to love this woman.

And love her we did. Any ninety-year-old deaf and blind woman who lives alone in the mountains with three dogs twice her size is worthy of inclusion in any book. We became fast friends, shared dinners and holidays, and argued ceaselessly about politics, religion, and F. Scott Fitzgerald. And the more time I spent with Wolfy and Molly, the more I realized that they were just a high-country version of Chaz and Sunshine, with one glaring exception: Wolfy and Molly had a foster child, a giant juvenile delinquent of a dog named Dirk.

A clueless, bumbling canine version of Inspector Clouseau, Dirk O'Dell was a two-year-old Great Dane/Doberman mix that Dorsa had rescued from a shelter in Julian. A true giant of an animal, Dirk had absolutely no awareness of his own size, and his random leaps from halfway across the room into my lap convinced me that he fancied himself a dachshund rather than a member of one of the largest breeds in the dog kingdom. Dirk was a mortal enemy of table lamps and flower vases—a drunken clown on a unicycle traveling from room to room could do less damage—and I constantly feared for Dorsa's fragile hips and body, always believing that it was just a matter of time before the one-hundred-pound Tasmanian devil would bowl over his diminutive owner. Miraculously, he never knocked her down—a statistic that I credit more to good fortune than to Dirk's sensitivity to her whereabouts.

Aside from retrieving brick-sized river stones from the backyard and laying waste to tastefully decorated coffee tables, Dirk loved to eat at least three or four books a week from Dorsa's extensive living-room library.

He was particularly fond of the classics—Dickens, Faulkner, Hemingway, and Steinbeck—and more than once I'd have to interrupt a meal of *A Tale of Two Cities* or some other priceless first printing. Eventually, we had to move all her first-edition, hard-cover copies from the lower to the upper shelves, where they would be out of reach of the oversized epicure.

On one occasion, Linda and I arrived to find Dirk snacking on an autographed copy of *When Good Dogs Do Bad Things*.

"How can you not love a dog that does that?" I asked.

"I have an issue of *Cat Fancy* in the car that he can have for dessert," Linda replied.

In total contrast, Wolfy and Molly, Dirk's reluctant stepparents, were model citizens. Wolfy was a majestic Irish wolfhound with a randy streak, and one could easily imagine him driving an MG convertible across the English countryside, occasionally sipping brandy from a silver snifter along the way. A perfect gentleman, he was a model of good behavior and always carried himself in fine form and posture. He had a perpetually jolly face and would bark only to lobby for a chest scratch or two. Like Chaz, he was very protective of his spouse, Molly, and would let visitors know in no uncertain terms if they were being disrespectful or playing too rough with his sweetheart.

Despite his professional manners, Wolfy did have a mischievous side, and once a month or so, in a rare departure from his usual conservative personality, he'd push open the front door and lead Molly and Dirk on a wild adventure throughout the countryside. Dorsa and I could never figure out where they went, the three of them often disappearing for five or six hours before returning out of breath and with tails wagging and tongues dangling in thirst. I always thought it was Wolfy's way of taking the family on a field trip, a monthly excursion to their favorite mountain meadow, where Molly could rest and relax under the canopy of a sprawling canyon oak while their supersized young hooligan ran wild. Whatever their destination, they all seemed quite happy when they returned, and their long absence always secured a good night's sleep for all.

Of the three, Molly was, by far, the most sensitive and reserved. A gentle Lab mix that often played the damsel in distress to Wolfy's dashing hero, she was the homely bookworm living in the rowdy frat house, with Dirk being the president and social director of the chapter. When things got too raucous, she'd retreat to her favorite corner by the fireplace, emerging only when Dirk went outside and the house calmed down. She spent most of her time in that cozy, out-of-the-way spot.

It must have been very difficult for Molly when Dirk arrived, upsetting and complicating her and Wolfy's quiet country lifestyle. Sometimes, when Dirk was busy in the yard mining rocks and peace was temporarily restored inside the house, I'd catch glimpses of Wolfy trying to console Molly, usually by encouraging her to come into the kitchen for a drink of water or to share a nap together on the comfy rug beneath the dining-room table. Wherever they ended up, Wolfy would always shield her body from the back door, where at any moment the one-dog wrecking crew might rush in. The only time I ever saw Wolfy raise his upper lip was when he felt Molly was threatened.

"He adores her," Dorsa would always say. "And she adores him."

We never talked much about *Island of the Blue Dolphins* during the year we lived in the mountains. Dorsa had been divorced from Scott for many, many years. She did surprise Hayden one day when they were making homemade toffee by giving her an autographed copy of the book. Hayden reciprocated by writing her sixth grade "People Who I Admire" report on our feisty and beloved neighbor.

"I wish I had known her for all my life," Hayden wrote.

Me, too.

woof

CHAPTER 13

Howdy

IT WAS A PLACE WE WALKED every Sunday morning, rain or shine. Spread out, stripped barren, and wide behind a brand-new elementary school, the old Wilson place was a prime piece of land that had been slated for development in the form of another personality-free neighborhood with no backyards and the pretentious name of Shady Grove. Of course, there was nary a tree to be found on the original hundred-acre homestead. Still, it was pretty much the last open space within walking distance from my house, and although privately owned, the preconstruction vacuum created by the six- to ten-month lag in the hard start time of the project made it the perfect place to bring your dog for a quick walk or off-leash run.

Personable to a fault, Howdy would make it a point to greet everyone on the trail, his easy-walk-up, friendly approach always putting people at ease and bringing a welcome smile to their faces. This particular morning the fields were empty except for two coyotes, a pair we often saw if we arrived early enough. Once Howdy spotted them, he would be gone.

It was the only time he didn't listen to me. With images of him being torn to shreds, I'd scream and yell and chase after him. But in time I gave up the chase. There was no stopping those kinds of missions and despite my fears, there never was a confrontation. It seemed that all they wanted

Howdy

to do was run together, a brief union between two worlds, one that was expanding and another that was shrinking. My border-collie-turned-wild-thing would eventually peel off and return to me, and I'd semiscold him for not listening, knowing that there are many things about my dogs that I'll never be able to control or understand.

That morning, on our way back to the car, I saw a dark figure walking toward us on the trail in the distance. As he got closer, Howdy started to walk up a bit as per usual to introduce himself and say hello. When the man was about twenty feet away, Howdy stopped dead in his tracks. He slowly lowered himself to the ground and started backing up in a semicircle as to be out of the direct path of the stranger. I had never seen him react to anyone or anything like that before.

As he drew closer, Howdy backed away even more and positioned himself firmly between the man and me. If ever there was a dark cloud hovering over a human being, it was this guy, and Howdy didn't move until the man, who was also talking to himself in the most frightening of tones, passed by.

"That man has done something really bad," I said to Howdy as we got in the car. I put the key in the ignition and noticed that my hand was shaking.

"Something really bad," I repeated out loud.

The next day they arrested a man in town who had raped a young girl.

TWO WEEKS AFTER CANYON DIED, I drove down to the shelter.

"Do you have any idea what you're looking for?" Linda asked when I returned.

"Not really," I said.

I sat down and wiped the dust off a book that was sitting on a table next to the couch. It was a book that Hayden had given to me for my birthday a few years before, *Nop's Trials*.

Maybe a border collie, I thought to myself.

I walked out to the driveway and picked up the local paper. I turned to the back and started thumbing through the classifieds. There was one ad under "Pets for Adoption."

FREE TO GOOD HOME. ONE-YEAR-OLD BORDER COLLIE. MALE. CALL AFTER 4 P.M.

I looked at my watch. It was 4:30. I ran inside and called the number. A man answered the phone.

"Yep, he's still here," he said. "Gotta find him a home 'cause we're movin' to Santa Fe next week."

I jumped in my truck and drove out to a ranch about twenty minutes away. As I pulled up the long, dusty drive lined with pepper trees and horse stables, I saw a black speck bounding down one of the more distant hillsides.

A tall man in a cowboy hat approached from a barn off to my right. I put the truck into park and slowly opened the door. A dog's face appeared from around the corner. I called to him. He wagged his tail, walked over, and put his head in my lap.

"Say hello to Howdy," the man said.

"I already have," I whispered through gathering tears.

A border collie it was.

The day after Howdy came home, I got a call from the vet's office. I could pick up Canyon's ashes anytime I wanted.

Since it was the first time I'd had a dog cremated, when I brought the small cedar box home, I wasn't quite sure what to do with it. Having heard how intelligent border collies were, I posed the question to Howdy.

"So, boy, what am I supposed to do? Open up the box and look inside or just put it up on the mantel?" I asked.

He looked at me in a way that would become so familiar for the next few years—a good-natured, levelheaded expression from a dog that, regardless of the situation, would always play his cards close to the vest.

I had been warned about adopting a border collie. He's going to need a job. You're going to have to run him every day. He's going to try to herd the kids. You better not have any cats. He's going to bond with just one family member and that's it.

One out of five isn't bad.

Howdy did, indeed, bond with me. I was sitting in the living room having just picked up Canyon's ashes, and I was crying very hard, the kind of tears that come when you lose a dog. And just like when I first pulled up in my truck at the ranch, Howdy came over and put his head in my lap. I looked down at him, and he looked back up at me in a way only border collies can. And that was it. We were bound together forever.

Regarding the other warnings, it became very clear early on that Howdy was not your typical border collie: *A job? No thanks; I'd rather be unemployed. Let's go for a run? Maybe tomorrow. Herd the kids? Sounds like a lot of work to me. Cats? Oh, is that what those are?*

Everything Howdy did was a study in reservation and understatement. Hearing that border collies were great Frisbee dogs, I took him into the backyard one afternoon and threw a perfectly retrievable toss, at which point he gave me a *what do you expect me to do with that?* kind of look, and then walked back into the house. I venture to say that there isn't a ball on earth that has found its way into the folds of his mouth, and the one time I took him to an agility course he fell asleep under the bleachers.

"He's a nerd," my then-teenage daughter would say.

It wasn't a totally inaccurate description of Howdy. Compared to other border collies, he was a bit of a geek. More introverted than outgoing, he displayed none of the characteristics associated with that typically wound-up herding breed. Aside from his wind sprints to run with the coyotes, he approached life in a comfortable gait, never rushing to or from anything. Sometimes I'd try to get him to play with me, roughhouse a bit in the living room with a chew toy or old sock. He'd try his best to please me with a couple of strained leaps and bounds before returning to his favorite spot on the couch. I finally realized that asking Howdy to play with me was like asking a classical pianist to open for Van Halen. In many ways, he was more greyhound than border collie—a dog that runs like the wind but prefers being a couch potato.

Like most geeks, he did have some unusual quirks. When it came to taking care of business, whether it was in the comfort of our backyard or on a hike down by the river, Howdy was brutally specific as to where he would go. It had to be up against some kind of bush or shrub, nothing too tall or short but medium in height. Like a customer testing easy chairs at a furniture store, I'd watch as Howdy might sniff and inspect a dozen bushes or so before settling on one, eventually backing into the branches and leaves like a cement truck dropping off a load at a construction site. It was a bizarre ritual, one I could never explain. The only thing I could figure was that it was his version of a bathroom, a somewhat private alternative to squatting in the middle of an open field.

"He's just weird," my daughter would insist.

While some dogs physically react to fear by shaking and panting, Howdy responded to such things as fireworks and thunderstorms in a much more "fragrant" manner.

"It sure smells a little gamey in here," a friend once remarked when Howdy hid behind the couch during a thunderstorm.

I asked my vet about the unusual odor during a routine checkup a few weeks later.

"That smell is coming from his anal glands," he said. "In some dogs, those glands will activate in response to a threat or fear."

"It really is a strong odor," I remarked.

"Well," he continued, "let's turn Howdy around, and I'll show you how to empty his anal glands at home."

Let me make this clear. I will give my dogs a bath. I will clip their toenails. I will brush their coats regularly. I will clean their ears and maybe even occasionally brush their teeth. But I will never go near anything that even vaguely resembles an anal gland. Some things are best left to professionals.

Howdy was adored by all our pets. Even the cats would curl up next to him on his favorite spot on our old leather couch, secure in the notion that he had no intention of chasing or bothering them. Cielo was especially fond of him, often sidling up to his shoulder as he walked around the yard, much like a pony escorting a thoroughbred racehorse in the post parade, occasionally nibbling or affectionately gnawing on Howdy's neck as he'd make the rounds on our spacious property.

When going for rides in my pickup, he was his usual practical self, choosing to curl up on the passenger side floor, rather than be bothered by the cars and trucks whirring by on the roads and highways. Even on the shortest trips to the market or the post office, he had no interest in sitting on the seat next to me. He was the calmest of all my passenger dogs and a pleasure to drive with, a very unusual combination given the state into which most dogs descend at the slightest hint of a ride in the car.

While he shied away from too much attention, he was always cordial and respectful when greeting guests in our home, never jumping up or pestering anyone for pats or scratches, calmly returning to his bed in the kitchen once the formalities had been completed.

"What a great dog," people would say. He sure was.

Not long after we got Howdy, the cat that I would measure all others against—my once-in-a-lifetime cat—Mitten, died. He had contracted feline AIDS in a fight with one of the feral cats in our neighborhood and had descended into a state of total dementia. It was a horrible illness, one that robbed him of both his independence and dignity. Having lost Canyon to cancer only a few years before, Mitten's death tore me apart. I don't think I've ever cried so hard for so long.

So when Howdy stopped eating, I barely had the will to bring him to the vet.

"He has some kind of growth in his intestines," the vet told me, pointing out the blockage on the X-ray. "It's in a very difficult spot, and there's no way of knowing if it's benign or malignant unless we operate."

A few weeks before, for some unexplainable reason, Howdy had eaten a large section of our living room carpet. I was hoping that the blockage was a result of that. We brought him in the next evening.

"Would you like to watch the operation?" the vet asked.

"Yes, I would," I said, remembering how Howdy had been there with me the days after I lost Canyon.

Our vet, Dr. Malcolm Jones, was an incredibly skilled surgeon, always willing to explain procedures and options both technically and practically. Like Howdy, he played his emotions very close to the vest. He was the perfect choice to operate on our beloved dog.

Being present at the operation wasn't as difficult as I expected. It's easy to imagine blood being everywhere, but once the vessels are clipped and secured, there is relatively little to be seen. What I did see was a fascinating puzzle of sorts—move this here, pull this back here, find the problem, remove it, and repair it. Any fear of getting sick was quickly overridden by the fact that this was my dog and I was willing to do anything for him. We were bound together forever.

Two days later, we got back the results. The tumor was malignant. It was lymphoma. Just like Canyon.

"But he's only seven," I whispered in disbelief.

Once again, we were faced with the same options. This time, we decided to try a new, somewhat experimental protocol. It was risky but promising.

The day that I picked Howdy up after the operation, for the first time in his life, he climbed up on the seat and sat next to me.

"I don't know how I can go through this again," I confessed.

For the whole ride home, Howdy never stopped looking at me. When we finally pulled into my driveway, I turned to give him my full attention.

"Don't worry," his tender eyes said.

There is no other dog in the world that looks at you in quite the same way as a border collie. So, true to his kind, he looked at me with as much love and affection as any man could wish for.

One week later, I had to go on a business trip to Arizona. Since we both loved the desert, I asked Linda to take off a few days from work and come along. Howdy was responding well to the early stages of his treatment, and Hayden, who was seventeen at the time, was going to stay at the house and take care of the pets while we were gone. She had many high school pals close by, and she could always call our dear friend, Connie Nelson, if she needed any help with anything or if there was an emergency.

"We'll be back on Sunday night," we told Hayden while going over the list of household responsibilities one more time. Howdy was resting in the corner on his bed in the kitchen.

"Take care of my boy," I said as we pulled out of the driveway.

The next morning, I got a call from Hayden.

"Dad, there's something's really wrong with Howdy." She sounded scared.

"What's the matter, honey?" I said, trying to stay calm.

"Oh, Daddy, please help me," she stammered. "I think he's really sick."

"Where is he, sweetheart?" I asked.

"I'm holding him in my lap," she said. "He can't get up, and he's breathing really fast. Oh, Daddy, please, you have to come home right away. . . ."

I took a deep breath and steadied myself.

"Hayden, I want you to rest Howdy's head on his blanket and get the list we left you on the counter. Dr. Jones's phone number is on there."

"Oh, Daddy, please help me!" she cried. "I don't know what to do. . . ."

"Everything is going to be OK," I tried to assure her.

Suddenly, there was silence on the end of the line.

"Hayden?"

"Oh, Daddy," she whispered through tears. "He's stopped breathing."

Howdy died in Hayden's arms on the kitchen floor at eleven o'clock that morning. I was five hundred miles away.

They say that you can measure the value of friends by whether they're willing to do things like help you move or if they'll get up in the middle of the night to give your car a jump. I'd like to add to that list asking someone to bury your dog when you're five hundred miles away. Which is exactly what Connie, Hayden, and three of her friends did that afternoon. In his favorite blanket. Under his favorite tree.

"I'm so sorry that you had to go through that," I told Hayden later that night.

"That's OK, Dad," she said. "Howdy knew that you couldn't handle being here this time."

As much as I'd like to believe that I can handle anything, especially when it comes to my dogs, Hayden was right. Sometimes I can't. And Howdy knew that, too.

My wife and I went for a walk in the desert that night. The air was fresh and fragrant from the short spell of rain earlier that afternoon, and the tall wisps of ocotillo were blooming reliably in clusters of red and orange.

"I think I'd like to live in the desert someday," I said.

"Me, too," Linda replied. "It's so quiet and clean."

I scoured the bare hillsides made beautiful by the setting sun for coyotes. There were none to be found.

"Let's go home," I said.

woof

CHAPTER 14

Osa and Cocoa

IF EVER THERE WERE A GROUP of dogs that could plead "canine racial profiling" in this country, it would be pit bulls. There is probably no more controversial topic when it comes to dogs than the American pit bull terrier. While rottweilers, mastiffs, and Dobermans have certainly had their share of bad press, they don't come close to evoking the kind of universal negative response garnered by this breed.

I know people who want them completely banned. I know people who couldn't live without them. I've known pit bulls that are as kind and docile as any other breed on the planet, and I've encountered others that would rip your arm out of its socket if given the right circumstances.

I've always approached pit bulls the same way I approach my horses—with a very clear understanding that at any given moment either could seriously injure me. It's not a personality, temperament, or intent issue, it's a cautiousness based primarily on pure physical strength and might. With any dog I meet, I try to use common sense and—an often-dismissed trait more commonly associated with man's best friend—natural instinct. It's this internal alarm that usually reveals itself with an uneasy feeling in my gut or a small voice that warns *better be careful here.* And it's usually right.

We had our share of pit bulls at the center but nowhere near the amount that the local pounds or animal-control shelters house at any given time. They were truly the lepers of the community, often passed by with barely a look from prospective individuals and families looking to adopt. I was just as guilty, spending as little time with them as I could, battling fear at every turn—never quite letting down my guard or prejudice. I cursed the fact that my perceptions had been contaminated by the news media and shameless shows such as *When Good Pets Go Bad*. It was only through an experience with another dog at the shelter that my whole opinion of pit bulls would change.

Ironically, the catalyst for my attitude shift was not a pit bull. Brandon was a Lassie-like, handsome, well-proportioned shepherd/collie mix with a medium-length feathery coat of appealing crèmes and tans. Sporting a breed combination that is usually quite friendly and personable, he had several shades of gold on his face, and his eyes were somewhat worrisome but approachable. Just two years old, he'd been at the shelter for about eight months, and unlike many dogs, he hadn't started to pace back and forth in his kennel, a pattern that is common among the longer-term residents. He'd just sit quietly in a corner and not move much, occasionally jumping up to train his sharp and pointed bark at someone he didn't like. As a result, he barked at me all the time.

For three months, I played missionary to Brandon's stubborn Indian. He didn't budge. I made little or no progress with him. Each time I even tried to get close to his kennel, his response was the same. He'd back up to his favorite corner, set his feet, offer me a toothy, low growl and then fire off a series of fierce and distinguished barks in my not-so-general direction. On days when I actually had to go inside his kennel to retrieve a blanket or a food dish, he would let me know of his displeasure very quickly. He'd back away even more and the hair on his back would rise up in deep protest. Each day with Brandon, I was nothing more than a vacuum-cleaner salesman standing in front of a freshly slammed door.

Usually, after repeated visits and long-term interaction, a dog will soften. I tried everything with Brandon. At first, I thought it might be a gender problem. But even though he seemed a bit more at ease with women, he was fine with the other male kennel techs. So I started hanging out with them and other people he liked. They even told him I was a great guy. He thought otherwise.

I tried bribing him with treats. He wouldn't go near them. I tried to play fetch with a ball. He looked at me as if I were an idiot. Going for the "tough love" approach. I decided to yell right back at him during his keenly directed barkathons. He just barked louder. Finally, I pretended that I didn't care anymore, feigning aloofness, hoping he might feel scorned. He didn't buy it. He always held his ground and never gave me an inch.

I touched him twice. Both times, he got a little too quiet and stood a little too still. I finally gave up my quest.

"Ever thought about trying the dog next door?" a vet tech suggested one day, knowing how little progress I'd made with Brandon. "She's the one that deserves the attention."

I'm embarrassed to say that I hadn't even considered visiting the dog next door to Brandon. Why? Because she was a pit bull—a very large pit bull.

"She's a Staffordshire and her name is Strawberry," the tech said as I read the adoption card above her kennel door. "They don't get anymore lovable than her. Why not give her a chance?"

Why not, you ask? Because I can fit my head in her mouth, that's why.

Up to that point, I had chosen to work with dogs that were familiar and that I felt most comfortable with—the black and yellow Labs, the golden retrievers, the huskies, and the mixed breeds. I had obviously chosen Brandon because his shepherd/collie blend reminded me so much of my childhood dog, Rusty.

But I hadn't yet been able to step out of my breed comfort zone when it came to devoting time to other dogs at the shelter. Strawberry would be the first.

"Think of it as 'pit bull rehab,'" one of the adoption counselors said.

The first day I ventured into Strawberry's kennel, you would have thought I'd been asked to remove a grizzly bear cub from the clutches of its mother on the Alaskan tundra. In retrospect, it must have seemed so silly to Strawberry, who sat there with her head tilted curiously to one side, as I talked baby talk and tiptoed about the kennel in what could have been a scene from a Richard Simmons exercise video.

"You're going to have to relax," the kennel tech said. "She's just a regular dog."

She was right. She *was* just a regular dog. The moment I stopped tap dancing and just stood there, Strawberry wandered over, tail wagging—a huge smile spreading across her big face—and plopped down on the floor right next to my feet. She then looked up at me as if to say, "Take a load off, big guy."

"Go ahead, sit down on the floor with her," the tech said. "Worst thing she might do is lick you to death."

I slid down along the concrete wall to the floor below, at which point Strawberry climbed in my lap and planted the biggest, sloppiest kiss I'd ever received from a dog. And a funny thing happened. I started to cry.

I have no idea why. Perhaps it was because of all the pit bulls I had ignored up to that point, ones that didn't make it, like Cherokee and Rex. Maybe it was because, at that moment, I realized that I couldn't save them all, including Brandon. Maybe it was just the years of fear melting away. Whatever it was, it quickly passed, much in part due to Strawberry—one of the jolliest, most loving dogs I've ever had the privilege to meet.

I wish I could have spent more time with her. But a few days after our get-together, she was adopted. To this day, if I close my eyes, I can still see her happy, gigantic face, a gift she left behind to help me see her brothers and sisters in a whole new light. Some ten years later, that new compassion would be put to the test.

When my new neighbor showed up at the front door, just a few weeks after we'd moved up to the high desert, and asked if I could take care of his horses and dog for a couple of days, I said sure.

"That's what neighbors are for," I replied. I asked him what kind of dog he had.

"A pit bull," he said.

Here we go.

Once again, I was proven foolish the next morning when I was greeted by one of the most engaging and fun-loving pups I've ever known.

"This is Osa," my neighbor said. "It means 'girl bear' in Spanish."

It sure did. Her ridiculously cute, six-month-old bear face looked like the grand prizewinner of a "Send us your most adorable pet snapshot" contest.

It turned out that Osa wasn't a purebred, but a pit bull/rottweiler/black Lab mix, a combination that seemed to bring out the better qualities of each breed—strength, tenacity, playfulness, and a healthy dose of goofball. We bonded immediately, a couple of chest scratches and a game of fetch securing the deal, and by the end of my first visit, as with most dogs of her temperament and flair, I wanted to take her home with me. I was curious to see how my border collie, Smokey, would react to this little ball of energy when I brought him with me the next day.

To avoid dominance and pack issues, it's always easier when introducing dogs for the first time if one is male and the other is female, and the results were no different with Smokey and Osa on their first "play day" together. And boy, did they play! After the standard tail-wagging introductions and physical once-overs were completed, they broke into a roughhouse romp that didn't end until we left half an hour later. They galloped and ran and hid behind trees, charging and slamming into each other chest high like mountain goats vying for mates, often collapsing into a dazed heap after their spirited collisions, before resuming their madcap game of tag and keep-away. Of course, Smokey was in herding-instinct overdrive, trying to cut off and corral the speedy Osa at every turn.

Exhausted, but never ready to give up, they'd eventually head over to the patio, grab a drink of water, and resume their battle in the form of a slow-motion sumo wrestling match, clutching and clinging to each other while standing on their back legs, both looking at me during these final rounds in hopes I might stop the match with an offer of a dog

Osa

bone or treat. It was the grandest of entertainment, and their antics never failed to make me roar with laughter.

For that first month, Osa had no other canine companions. Consequently, she hated to see Smokey and me leave and would often wrap her legs around me in protest as I unlatched the gate to head back home. Later, I'd see her frolicking about, making the best of the fact that she was alone, flipping old sneakers recruited as doggy toys high into the air and chasing crows that dared to land on her sandy playground.

While Osa didn't have any brother or sister pups to play with, she did have another four-legged pal to help occupy her time: a twelve-year-old quarter horse named Angel.

I'm convinced that Osa viewed the easygoing Palomino mare as just an oversized yellow Labrador retriever. She'd constantly try to get Angel to play with her, running in circles underneath her long legs, jumping up and down in front of her, trying to get her attention. Angel was a model of patience and tolerance, usually resolving the situation by lying down to take a nap. Osa, unfazed by the move, would usually curl up right beside her and grab a couple of winks as well. Come dinnertime, whether it was sweet feed, grain, timothy pellets, alfalfa, carrots, or apples, Osa would always join Angel for a bite or two at the food station, finishing off the meal by sharing a flake or two of Bermuda-grass hay together. It was an unusual and endearing friendship and an affirmation of their innate kindness and loving dispositions. And to see a dog of pit bull and rottweiler blood cordially share a flake of hay with a horse four times its size kind of throws a monkey wrench into the stereotypical profile of those breeds. Like Strawberry, Osa was instrumental in helping me dismantle any broad generalities regarding pit bulls.

After a month or two of my periodically caring for Osa, everything would soon change because of a new addition to her animal family.

"Sure, what did you get?" I asked my neighbor, as he inquired about helping out with the pets for the upcoming week while he was out of town.

"Another pit bull," he said.

I must be on some kind of pit-bull initiation or intervention list, I thought to myself.

"He's a pup, and he doesn't like men too much," he continued. "If he growls at you, just give him a kick in the ass."

"What's his name?" I asked, as he stepped off my front porch.

"Cocoa," he said.

So the next morning, sans Smokey, I headed across the street to meet Cocoa. Osa, who was delighted to see me as usual, greeted me at the gate full of cheer and anticipation.

"Where's your new pal?" I asked out loud to the bear-faced puppy while unlocking the gate. I received my answer quickly when around the corner of the garage lumbered a broad-shouldered, jumbo-headed battleship of a dog.

"Now, that's what I call a pit bull," I mumbled to myself.

Although still a puppy, Cocoa was a textbook example of an American pit bull terrier. All muscle, brawn, and girth, he approached me with the

Cocoa

swagger of a pumped-up and buffed-out bodybuilder after a two-hour power workout. We got off to a rocky start.

"Hey there, buddy," I said, while slipping inside the gate.

With his whiplike tail standing straight up, he backed up, lowered his head, and gave me the kind of growl reserved for horror films. Osa, totally oblivious to Cocoa's dubious welcome wagon, looked at me with her happy head, a bit confused as to why we weren't playing ball already.

"So you don't like men, eh?" I said, while trying to take a circular route to the garage, where the hay and dog food was kept for Angel and Osa.

Cocoa watched my every move, jumping back at the slightest indication of an approach, growling and raising his upper lip the whole time. The only thing I had going for me was that he was a puppy and I could have handled him if he really tried anything. Still, I decided to go with a different tactic.

There's no faster or more efficient way to get a dog's attention than with a treat. And since I'd been bringing over some very tasty dog bones for Osa every morning, I decided to highlight that exchange even more, focusing all of my attention on giving Osa a treat while pretending that Cocoa didn't exist. This combination of praise and biscuits coupled with the irresistible crunchy sounds coming from Osa's mouth proved to be too much for my little man-hating friend. He slowly wandered over to investigate.

"Want a cookie, Cocoa?" I said in my sweetest voice.

When he was still a good five feet away, I reached out my hand, leaving plenty of room between the end of the dog bone and the tips of my fingers, and called to him again. He moved a little closer, and then, like a wild squirrel accepting a handheld peanut for the first time, he grabbed the prize and ran away.

We repeated this routine four more times, and then I went home.

"See you tomorrow, kids," I said while locking the gate. Nothing like running a preschool for pit bulls.

The next day I returned, armed with more biscuits and a new strategy. Like training a young horse, Cocoa was going to have to work a little harder to get his reward today.

Upon hearing the first jangles of the gate chain, Osa, as usual, came galloping around the corner. But this time, she had a little pit bull chugging along, right beside her.

"Well, well, well," I said. "What do we have here?"

I hesitate to say that I witnessed a minor miracle that morning, but there was Cocoa, standing right next to Osa, tail wagging, with a big dopey smile on his face. I decided to break the ice a little differently and promptly gave them each a treat through the chain-link fencing on the gate.

Once inside, Cocoa accepted the rest of his treats a bit brusquely, more out of awkwardness at being hand-fed for the first time, I suspect, than from aggression. He still recoiled at any attempt to touch or pet him, but he had now taken up the sport of bumping into my legs as I fed the horses and filled water and food bowls. As strange as it might seem, I honestly believe it was a safe way for him to make human contact. I think he was also imitating Osa, who loved nothing more than to wrap her paws around your ankles if you gave the slightest indication of leaving.

The next day, I introduced a ball into the mix. With Cocoa regularly banging into me and sticking closer each day, I could see that he wanted to play with the ball but didn't know how. Each time Osa would retrieve it, I'd pick up the ball and literally place it inside Cocoa's big, clueless mouth. He was happy that he finally had the ball, but he wasn't quite sure what to do about it, so I'd urge him to run away and keep it from Osa. But he'd just look at me, triumphantly wagging his tail, totally oblivious as to what I was asking him to do, at which time Osa would walk over and matter-of-factly take it out of his mouth. It was a scene right out of *One Flew Over the Cuckoo's Nest,* with me playing Jack Nicholson's McMurphy to Cocoa's Chief, all the while yelling, "Keep the ball in your mouth, Chief! Keep the ball in your mouth!"

On day four, every time Cocoa banged or bumped into me while I was doing my rounds, I tried to sneak in a scratch or two, nothing too obvious, just a casual, barely noticeable rub on his shoulder or neck. He was also beginning to accept his treats more gently, and at one point he even let me pet the top of his head, closing his eyes in approval for a brief second, until snapping back to cautious attention. It was at that moment that I saw the conflict in his eyes, a look that clearly said, *I'm not supposed to let you pet me.*

A plane passed high above us in the bright morning sky. Another beautiful day was unfolding in the high desert, so far away from the troubled streets of south Los Angeles where Cocoa had first been introduced to the world. I picked up the old softball that Osa had dropped by my feet.

"OK, Cocoa, let's try this again," I said.

woof

CHAPTER 15

Rickel and Sandy

IF YOU LIVE IN THE CITY, suburbs, or country and you own a dog, sooner or later you're going to be introduced to the dogs in your neighborhood. You may meet some of them at the ends of assorted colors of leashes, at a doggie park, or up close nose to nose while on your daily morning walks around the block. Others you'll get to know from a distance, those barking from behind fences or inside big living-room bay windows. Some you'll get to know on a first-name basis, while others you may see or pass by for years without ever learning their names—forever remaining anonymous but familiar at the same time.

Two dogs from two different neighborhoods that have left their marks on my life. Two little girls have adored each. One's still fresh in my heart; the other is from a long time ago.

Some twenty years have passed since we moved from the suburbs of New Jersey to the rolling hills of Warwick. By the end of our first month in our new house, most of the local dogs had already stopped by at least once to check out the latest additions to their neighborhood. Many just passed on through. Some stopped by to sniff around and deposit an opinion or two about the place and its new occupants.

There was one little Lab who gladly decided to pay us a visit—a free-spirited pup whose cheerful attitude had obviously earned him a position in the canine wing of Warwick's "Welcome Wagon." His name was Rickel.

Named after a very popular chain of home-improvement stores at the time (where his owners found him), he wandered into our yard one spring afternoon, closely followed by a whimsical little girl in a pink dress carrying a large shoebox.

"Hi, my name is Heidi," she said sweetly. "I was wondering if your dogs would like to join Rickel for his one-year-old birthday party." She placed the shoebox down on our wooden picnic table and opened the top. Inside was what looked like about seven cans of dog food molded into a meat-loafish birthday cake. "I made him a cake," she said proudly. Dry pieces of chow and colorful dog bones carefully inscribed the words "Happy Birthday, Rickel" on top.

"We can make it a 'new neighbor' party, too, if you'd like?" Heidi smiled.

"Deal," I said. I couldn't help but think what a nice new friend Heidi would be for our daughter, Hayden.

"I'm sure Squeeze and Brody would love to be a part of Rickel's birthday party," my wife said, as Heidi pulled some small paper plates out of her jacket pocket.

"Can I invite the cats, too?" I asked.

"That's probably not a good idea," Heidi said while slicing the "cake" into thick servings. "Rickel likes to eat cats."

"Oh, well, in that case, maybe that's not such a good idea," I replied, as Rickel sniffed my shoes. He was a very likable yellow Lab mix with a happy, eager face.

"Well, he doesn't really eat cats," she continued, while concentrating on spooning the slices onto the paper plates. "But he sure likes to chase them up trees!"

Linda let Brodie and Squeeze out the front door, and they quickly ran over to check out their new neighbor. With Rickel being male and both Brodie and Squeeze being female, the formalities were brief and nonconfrontational, and soon the girls were giving him a tour of the farm.

After the birthday cake was evenly distributed, we called the dogs back over, and they jumped up onto the redwood picnic benches. Naturally, Heidi insisted that we all sing "Happy Birthday" to the guest of honor.

"OK, everybody, dig in!" Heidi announced after we'd all finished singing. And dig in they did, as all three dogs inhaled their "cake" in two or three bites. When it was time to clean up, Heidi appeared a little down. I wondered what was wrong.

"I didn't have enough money to buy him a new collar," she said slowly.

"Well, I can't remember the last time anyone made a birthday cake for their favorite dog. That was very special, Heidi," Linda said, attempting to make the little girl feel better. It worked. Heidi looked up and smiled. She looked pretty in her pink party dress.

Two weeks later, on her ride home from school, a pickup truck ran a stop sign and slammed into the side of the car that Heidi was a passenger in. She had been sitting in the back seat and was killed instantly. I met her father at the bottom of the driveway twenty minutes after he had received the phone call. There are no words to describe the heartache.

A year later, we had to sell the farm. We had fallen upon some financial hard times and just couldn't keep up with the payments. As a stopgap measure, we rented a small house about five miles away—a little cabin on five acres backing up to some woods and overgrown cornfields. It was a wild, out-of-the-way place, and we were frequently visited by herds of white-tailed deer, flocks of wild turkey, and other assorted critters.

One Saturday morning, as I was raking leaves, I heard some rustling at the far end of the yard and saw a medium-size dog emerge from the brambly brush surrounding our property. He was dirty and a little beat-up, signature signs of a country dog that loved to wander and explore. I called to him, and he trotted right over. He had a happy, eager face.

"Rickel?" I said out loud in disbelief.

Wagging his tail in warm recognition, he sat down by my feet and leaned up against my leg. How he'd found us, God only knows. I cupped his head in my hands and looked at his face, so much older than I'd remembered, and there was a newfound wilt to his gentle eyes. I sat with him next to a pile of fallen maple leaves for a good while, scratching his chest and staring out over the orange-and-gold-covered hillside. Fall was here, and soon that same radiant hillside would be cold and barren.

"Are you thirsty, boy?" I asked, while standing up to brush off my jeans. He gave me a hopeful look, the kind reserved for such silent requests, so I went inside the house to fetch my weary nomad a bowl of cool water. Brodie and Squeeze flew by me as I opened the back door, and they enthusiastically greeted him, tails wagging curiously as they started their mandatory tour of the yard, sniffing and marking swing sets and fence posts along the way. They played and ran around for about an hour, and then Rickel disappeared back into the brush. I never saw him again. It would be a very long time before a dog that wasn't mine would leave such an impression on me.

SHE JOINED SMOKEY AND ME one morning on our walk. The next day, she decided to tag along as well. The following morning she was waiting for us at the top of her driveway.

"By week's end I fully expect her to join us for breakfast," I told Linda.

If there's one dog in our new neighborhood that is welcome to join Smokey and me anytime or anywhere, it's Sandy. And while it's hard to say if we've adopted her part-time or she's adopted us (I think it's probably somewhere in between the two), I'm pretty sure that Sandy has chosen us as her primary daycare provider.

I think one of the things that my mother is most proud of is that when my brother and I were growing up, all our friends wanted to

Sandy

hang out at our house. We had a basketball court in the driveway and a finished basement with Ping-Pong tables and hockey games, and I think everyone felt safe and comfortable inside the lively and loving walls of our home. Whether it was watching the Knicks or Rangers on TV or playing wiffleball in the street, there was always something to do at 17 Orchard Road.

"I think you're carrying on the same tradition at your house with dogs and cats," my mom said sweetly when I told her about Sandy.

Sandy's daily calling to hang out at our house is a totally newfound behavior that, in an eleven-year-old female, her owner deems "a bit senile in nature." Frankly, I think that, as a former Wyoming ranch dog, she just longs for her working days on the open range. And with Smokey and me passing by her house most every morning, there is no way she can resist the temptation to hit the road with us and run wild like the old days.

And what a joy she is to have with us every day! Ridiculously obedient and respectful, she listens like few dogs I have ever known, always swift in her willingness to come at my slightest command. She's a tough, middle-aged girl and, despite her inherent sweetness, definitely not a pushover and will quickly raise her upper lip and growl in protest if Smokey gets in her face, a message that he has willingly accepted without losing any enthusiasm to run with her at any given chance.

And boy, can they run! To watch two border collies run flat out, side by side, is a wonder of natural dynamics and design. Occasionally, they'll get into a one-on-one herding match, racing around the fringes of our property in broad circles, constantly looking to cut each other off, never allowing more than a step or two's advantage between them. It is the grandest of entertainment, and I never tire of watching them play together.

While she is impeccably disciplined, Sandy does have her occasional weak moments; namely, when it comes to chasing crows and rabbits. When either come into her sights, there's no stopping her. There is no clicker, whistle, or reprimand that will change her directive, very similar to when my sugar or chocolate jones kicks in—I'm going to the nearest 7-Eleven for a Mounds bar, and nothing is going to stop me. She'll eventually peel off and return to me, totally unaware of the fact that she never had a prayer of catching that crow or rabbit but very pleased by her efforts nonetheless.

And like many dogs, she can't quite figure out what to do with our horses, and her herding instinct only seems to add to her frustration. While Smokey is content to just stare at my mustang and Linda's Anglo-Arabian, Sandy will often run around in circles, constantly looking to me, as border collies always do, for guidance and instruction.

"You're from Wyoming," I'll say good-naturedly. "Do they look like sheep to you?"

She'll whine and spin around in protest, barely able to contain her natural urge to nip at hooves and heels shuffling around feed buckets and water troughs. Luckily, a ball thrown in her direction is usually enough to break the spell, setting off a wild game of competitive fetch that usually ends up with both Smokey and Sandy collapsing on the front porch in a heap. I'll join them on the steps for a mutual breather and pull them close. Two border collies by my side, as the sun slowly begins to set—there's no better way to end the day.

Before it gets dark, Linda and I will walk Sandy home. Sandy's owner and his two little girls, Melissa and Elizabeth, will usually greet us in the driveway. We always bring Smokey along for the short trip down the block.

"What's your doggie's name?" the younger one, Elizabeth, always asks.

"That's Smokey," I'll tell her, as he generously showers her with kisses.

"Thanks for watching our girl," Sandy's owner says.

"No problem," I reply. "She's a pleasure to have around."

As we turn to head back home, a little voice calls out from the front porch.

"Do you love my Sandy?" Melissa asks.

I turn around to see a little girl hugging one of the sweetest dogs I've ever known.

"Yes," I'll say. "I love your Sandy very much."

woof

CHAPTER 16

Smokey

EVERY TIME I LOSE A DOG, it's like falling off a horse. There's a part of me that doesn't want to get another or get back on. And the longer I wait, the less likely I am to do either.

A few years back, I decided to quit surfing and learn how to ride something new. I traded in my surfboard for an Appaloosa/mustang gelding named Bob. It was a difficult but smart move. The cold Pacific Ocean waters were starting to wreak havoc with the broken bones and fractured joints left over from my youth. It also was something Linda and I could do together. She's been riding horses for most of her life.

Not long after Howdy died, I got thrown from my horse for the first time. Linda and I were riding on a busy suburban park trail when a dog charged an adjoining fence at the top of a ridge. My horse spooked and bolted downhill toward an area of thick brush and trees. When we reached the bottom, he cut sharply to the left and I went right. Next thing I knew, I was airborne.

I must have flown a good ten feet before I landed on a large rock that was half-buried in the dirt. I remember lying on the ground, watching my horse run around, both of us scared and disoriented, thinking that I probably should get up and grab his reins.

But I couldn't move. Getting thrown when you're fifty is a helluva lot different from when you're thirty. So I looked over at my corner and my trainer (Linda), who told me to stay down on the ground. I took the eight-count, all the while talking to my horse that was, thankfully, staying close by. I finally staggered to my knees, then to my feet, and walked over and took hold of his reins.

"Are you all right?" Linda asked.

"I think so," I said.

I wanted to tell her that I was fine, but I couldn't lie. I had little or no feeling from my right hip down to my knee, and I was shaking from fear.

"Maybe I'll just walk him back to the stables," I said.

"No, you won't," Linda said. "You're going to get right back on."

While every bone in my sore body wanted to turn my back on the time-tested axiom of "when you fall off your horse, dust yourself, and etc., etc.," I knew that I didn't have a choice. Especially if I wanted to ride again.

And so I got back on.

Later that afternoon, when I got home, I limped out to the driveway and picked up the local paper, knowing that if I waited any longer, I would never get another dog. I turned to the back and started thumbing through the classifieds. There was one ad under "Pets for Adoption."

One-year-old purebred border collie needs good home. All shots and papers. $100. Call after 5:00 p.m.

Another border collie it was.

The following morning, I drove to a different ranch, this one about an hour away in horse country. The woman I spoke to on the phone was a breeder, and the dog that was up for adoption had recently been returned.

"The owner said he wasn't aggressive enough in the field," she explained.

As I turned into the long, dusty driveway leading up to the ranch, I decided that his shortcomings in the field might be a good thing, especially since I had no plans to buy sheep anytime soon.

A very likable woman greeted me as I stepped out of my pickup.

"Are you here to see Smokey?" she asked.

"I sure am," I said.

"Well, come around back, and I'll introduce you to him," she replied.

I followed her around the corner of her cozy clapboard-sided cottage, down a hill, and past some very nice horses.

"Do you breed horses as well?" I asked.

"Thoroughbreds," she said. "That one's getting ready to foal any day now."

She was a beautiful chestnut mare, made all the more magnificent in the hazy morning sun that was rising up behind her.

"I got thrown yesterday for the first time," I said, wanting to tell her the whole story in detail. I didn't get the chance.

"Well, it's like they say," she said matter-of-factly. "When it comes to gettin' thrown, it's not a question of if. It's only a question of when."

"Well, if that's the case, I'm glad I got that first one out of the way," I laughed.

"It won't be the last one, either," she promised.

She was right. Two months later, I got thrown again.

"Next time, just go along for the ride," Linda said.

Whether you adopt a dog or rescue a horse (which I did with my mustang), there are always risks involved. People can be less than honest about a horse's history, and rarely do you find a dog at a shelter that's been surrendered or returned for *good* reasons. That said, sometimes we choose our dogs, and sometimes they choose us. Most times it falls somewhere in between the two. The uncanny coincidence of finding another ad for another border collie in the same newspaper that I found Howdy got me to the ranch that morning. The rest was up to me.

"There's Smokey," the young woman said, pointing to an outdoor kennel where a young dog sat alone.

Regardless of his personality or behavior, just the sight of him sitting all by himself immediately shifted the Vegas odds that I would take him down to even money.

Smokey

She unlocked the kennel, and Smokey bolted out. He gave me the quickest of sniff-overs and then headed straight for the horses.

"He loves the horses," she added. "He's pretty good with them, too."

I watched as the one-year-old castoff ran up and down the fence line, finally settling his attention on the pretty pregnant mare.

"He'll sit there for an hour and just stare at her," the woman continued. "I think that was his problem in the field. He was perfectly content to stare at the sheep instead of herd them."

I realized that I was just moments away from adopting a border collie version of Canyon.

"I'll let you guys hang out for a bit while I go make some phone calls," she said. "There's no rush . . . take your time."

She walked back up to the house, and I headed over to the corral. Smokey was lying belly tight to the ground, his entire being locked onto the mare. There was drool hanging from the side of his mouth. I determined that it was not from hunger but from the fact that he probably hadn't swallowed in an hour.

"Time to break the spell," I mumbled to myself. "Come here, Smokey."

He immediately ran over and sat down at my feet. What I saw was a very young, unsure puppy, willing to please and ready to run. I also noticed one more thing.

When I asked for his attention, he looked me straight in the eye.

Of all the things I look for when adopting a dog, it's their willingness to give me their attention when I ask for it. Not a fleeting glance or brief acknowledgement of my existence but a firm, locked look into my eyes, even if it's only for a few moments.

There was a dog that wandered into our yard one day. He was one of the "brown ones," a shepherd/one-hundred-other-breeds mix that was handsome and perpetually restless. It was hard to determine whether he was lost or abandoned, as he had no collar or tags.

Once I go through the proper channels of trying to locate a stray's possible owners, any dog that shows up at my door has a good chance of becoming a part of our family. Such was the case with this dog. He was extremely friendly and a bit unruly, but I attributed that mostly to the fact that he still had some puppy in him. But there was a problem—I couldn't get his attention.

No matter how hard I tried, he wouldn't look me in the eye for more than a second or two without becoming irreversibly distracted. The next day he was gone. He had jumped the backyard fence in the middle of the night, and we never saw him again.

Once I got that look from Smokey's eyes, I knew we had a chance. It wouldn't be easy. But we had a chance. So I took him home.

Although he looked much different from Howdy, I'm sure that when Smokey first walked into the house, the other animals thought that Howdy had risen from the dead. Cielo walked over and immediately started gnawing on Smokey's neck and shoulder like the good old days. Smokey handled her spontaneous outburst of affection quite well. Our nineteen-year-old semiburned-out hippie cat, Rainbow, was totally confused—particularly when the Howdy-clone decided to make her his twenty-four-hour-a-day object of desire.

"Here comes the drool," I said to Linda as he was wrapping up his first one-hour staring session with Rainbow.

"At least we'll always know where he is," she replied dryly.

I've heard of other border collies myopically focusing on things for hours, but it's still one of the most bizarre behaviors I've ever seen. It's not as if Rainbow is moving about the house. About 90 percent of the time Smokey is staring at her while she's fast asleep. When she finally does get up to stretch or grab a bite to eat, he'll follow her wherever she goes, never getting closer than three feet. Once she returns to the couch for a nap, Smokey will resume his drooling vigil.

"Why can't I have a normal dog?" I'll wail sometimes.

"Because you can't walk away from the not-so-normal ones," Linda says.

She's right. I can't.

My mother once told me, as I was grieving the loss of one dog and debating about getting another, that if I cared that much, to hurt that much, then there's a dog out there that needs a home like ours. I've never forgotten that.

Apart from his obsession with watching cats sleep, Smokey becomes completely possessed at the sight of a lawn sprinkler, particularly the ones that rotate in a circle. To this point, he has killed three and seriously injured two.

Water flowing from the end of garden hoses is another favorite attention-grabber, as is any activity that has to do with a rake or a shovel. As a result, you can count on Smokey stalking and herding all three items during the once-routine chores of washing the car, cleaning up leaves, or digging holes. And his fondness for water goes well beyond the garden hose. On hot summer afternoons, it's not uncommon to find him taking a dip in the horses' one-hundred-gallon water trough. Most times, all you can see is his head.

"What kind of dog is that?" a neighbor, seeing Smokey in the water, once asked.

"Part border collie, part hippopotamus," I said.

Despite his hippo tendencies and staring problem, I am constantly amazed by Smokey's intelligence and acute awareness of the world around him. I'm pretty sure it's a border collie thing. His ability to associate and interpret the most commonplace sounds with specific activities is remarkable. While many dogs can easily associate the jangle of a leash with a walk or the sound of a can opener with an imminent meal, Smokey has the ability to connect the dots like no other dog I've owned.

By listening to the way I reach into the doggie jar for a bone, he can determine whether I'm getting a treat for just Cielo and him or if I'm grabbing an extra couple of treats for Osa and Cocoa across the street prior to a hike together. Depending on each, he'll either come to the kitchen or wait for me by the front door.

Every night, regardless of where he is in the house, the sound of my computer shutting down immediately sends him to his soft bed in the laundry room. The most distant howl of a coyote will put him on the highest alert, and I swear he can tell whether I'm staying home or heading into town just by the kind of T-shirt I put on in the morning.

All of these things tell me that I have an intensely hypersensitive dog. At times he reminds me of some of the dogs that didn't make it at the shelter, the Fraziers and Parson Browns of the world that were so painfully aware of and so easily overwhelmed by a world that never seemed to stop tumbling in around them. I'm glad I got another chance to save one.

When we moved up to the high desert, an endless system of riding and hiking trails opened up to us, many of which we can access right off our property. And while I still go on my regular morning walks with Smokey, he can now add the title of "trail dog" to his résumé. It's the best of both worlds for my tireless pal. And to go on an early-morning horseback ride with your best dog by your side is damn near close to heaven on earth.

On one of our first trail rides with Smokey off the new property, my horse, Bob, spooked at a plastic bag stuck in a chain-link fence that happened to rustle in the wind as we walked by. Like many horses, Bob was positive that the plastic bag was an alien creature and its only reason for being there was to kill him. This time, Bob spun around to the right. And I went along for the ride.

woof

Epilogue

NOT LONG AGO, I CAME across a young mother at a local bookstore. She had three children in tow, all under the age of five. The oldest daughter was looking for a book about dogs.

"We're getting a ridgeback," the girl proudly announced. "And I'm looking for a book about them."

"Oh, we *are*, are we?" her mother laughed, turning toward me. "Frankly, I don't know what we're going to get. Everyone says, 'Get a Labrador or a golden retriever—they're so great with kids,' but my husband wants a Ridgeback . . . and I don't really want a little dog. What do you think?"

Hmmm, let's see. Last week on our morning walk, a ridgeback knocked the usually nimble Smokey flat on his backside during an impromptu play session in front of our house. Canyon, my golden retriever, and Squeeze, my Labrador, were both terrified of kids. And Cielo, the one dog that has always been the lowest maintenance and the best with children of all ages, is a fox terrier we smuggled across the Mexican border. So, unless she wants to head down to Tijuana or accept the fact that all of the purebred dogs in my life have routinely "colored outside the lines," I'm either the best or the worst person to ask for advice right now, I thought to myself.

"Have you thought about going down to the shelter?" I asked.

"My husband mentioned it," she said.

"Why don't you head down to the shelter this weekend and check out some of the brown ones?" I suggested.

"What are 'the brown ones'?" she laughed.

"You know, the dogs that are about a hundred different breeds mixed together," I said. "That's a good place to start."

"The brown ones, huh?" she said, as her youngest daughter, growing impatient, tugged on her arm.

I wanted to tell her about Brody and Margarita and Champ and Yellow Dog. But I knew they'd all be there.

One way or another.

woof

About the Author

Gary Shiebler is an award-winning singer and songwriter who has produced and written for such country-music legends as Tanya Tucker, Bobby Bare, George Jones, Patty Loveless, Merle Haggard, and Porter Wagoner, to name a few. His love for animals—especially dogs, cats, and horses—and his work as a humane educator at the nationally recognized Helen Woodward Animal Center in Southern California inspired him to write *The Power of Paws* and *The Power of Purrs*. He lives with his wife Linda and daughter Hayden in Anza, California, with a host of critters that includes two horses, two dogs, two cats, and one cranky cockatiel.

woof